SUPREME QUOTES:
SURPRISING QUOTATIONS IN SUPREME COURT OPINIONS

by
Evan J. Roth

William S. Hein & Co., Inc.
Getzville, New York
2022

Publishers' Cataloging-in-Publication Data

Names: Roth, Evan J., 1960- compiler.

Title: Supreme quotes : surprising quotations in Supreme Court opinions / by Evan J. Roth.

Description: Getzville, New York : William S. Hein & Co., Inc., 2022. | Includes indexes.

Identifiers: ISBN: 978-0-8377-4255-7 | LCCN: 2022935057

Subjects: LCSH: United States. Supreme Court--Officials and employees--Quotations. | Judges--United States--Quotations. | Law--United States--Quotations. | Judicial opinions--United States-- Language. | Legal opinions--United States--Language. | LCGFT: Quotations.

Classification: LCC: KF8742.A35 R68 2022 | DDC: 347.73/2603--dc23

Printed in the United States of America

This volume is printed on acid-free paper.

DEDICATION

To those whose quotes I miss the most:
Ann Roth, George Roth,
Florence Roth, and Eric Roth

ACKNOWLEDGMENTS

I would like to acknowledge those who helped me so much along the way.

First and foremost, I thank Kathy Holub and the *Maine Bar Journal* for providing a welcome home for my Supreme Quotes column. I am especially grateful for Kathy's support providing the layout and graphics and prominent placement that helped make the column so popular.

I thank my dear friend, Assistant U.S. Attorney Margaret Groban, who for many years encouraged me to write this book. I also thank Margaret for helping me develop the idea of including a narrative explanation for each Supreme Quote.

I thank Mark Srere, Jayne Jerkins, and Jeff Balch, for their support and encouragement and suggestions upon reviewing the manuscript.

I thank retired U.S. Attorney Paula Silsby, for always challenging me to do my best work, and for supporting my Maine Bar Journal column.

I thank the Honorable W. Eugene Davis, of the U.S. Court of Appeals for the Fifth Circuit, for choosing me as his Law Clerk, and for acceding to my one memorable request to include a one-liner in a judicial decision.

I thank the Honorable James Morris, the late Virginia Bergan Morris, and Josephine D'Ambrosia, for introducing me to the law at the Brighton Town Court.

I thank the U.S. Merit Systems Protection Board for supporting this project.

I thank Mika Holliday Lentz for her inspired archival work.

I thank my family, Neil Roth, Jorian Roth, David Roth, Marisa Roth, Sara Page, Cassandra Blattner, David Blattner, Jim Page, and Louise Page, for their love and support.

I thank my dear friends, Andy Kindfuller, Dan Lawton, Elizabeth Bennett, Eric Rait, Elizabeth Willen, Janet Brooks, Marty Rosenberg, Sara Snow, Anders Granberg, Heather Donnelly, Anna Phillips, and the late Jack Grosslein, for supporting me through thick and thin.

I thank Katherine Ward, my love, for supporting me through this project, for encouraging me to submit the manuscript for publication, and for saving my life in so many ways. I love us.

And most of all I thank my wonderful boys, Jackson, Anders and Gareth, my beloved "JAG Corps," who support me, inspire me, humor me, and make me so proud—even when they scare the living daylights out of me as they mimic Calvin and Hobbes and jump out from their secret hiding spots.

Evan J. Roth
December 13, 2021
Golden, Colorado

DISCLAIMER

The views expressed are those of the author
and do not necessarily represent
the position of the U.S. Merit Systems Protection Board
or the United States government.

TABLE OF CONTENTS

PREFACE

In the Summer of 2009, I began to write "Supreme Quotes" as a regular column for the *Maine Bar Journal*. The format was the same as the individual entries in this book: I began each column with an unusual quotation from a Supreme Court opinion, and then I described how and why the quotation was used. It was a hit.

The idea for the column, and ultimately for this book, developed from two threads in my life. The first was my lifelong love of popular quotations. Since I was a teenager, I have been fascinated with books like *Bartlett's Familiar Quotations*, which offer so much wisdom in so little space. The other thread was my 35-year career using computerized legal research as a Judicial Law Clerk for the U.S. Court of Appeals for the Fifth Circuit, as a litigation associate for the law firm of Williams & Connolly, as an Assistant U.S. Attorney for the District of Maine, and now as an Administrative Judge for the U.S. Merit Systems Protection Board.

This book weaves together those two threads.

PERMISSIONS

From page 107: Translation of Virgil reprinted under fair use per Penguin Random House from *The Aeneid* (Shadi Bartsch trans., lines 159–161, p. 8 (2021)).

From page 109: Quotation from Kurt Vonnegut's "Harrison Bergeron," reprinted under fair use per Penguin Random House from *Animal Farm and Related Readings* (McDougal Littell, p. 129 (1997)).

From pages 111–15: Select Glossary definitions reprinted by permission of Thomson Reuters from *Black's Law Dictionary 5th ed.* (West Pub. Co. 1979).

INTRODUCTION

In 2008, when *60 Minutes'* Leslie Stahl interviewed Supreme Court Justice Antonin Scalia, she asked why his judicial opinions often included quotations from history, literature, and popular culture. Justice Scalia answered: "It makes the opinion interesting, which might induce somebody to read it."

Supreme Quotes is the first popular reference book to collect the surprising quotations used by the Supreme Court Justices to make their opinions more interesting.

The quotes are from satirists (Joseph Heller, George Orwell, Mark Twain, and Kurt Vonnegut), and philosophers (Albert Camus and the Dalai Lama). The sources include actors (Alan Alda, Humphrey Bogart, and Clark Gable), playwrights (Robert Bolt, Ira Gershwin, and William Shakespeare), politicians (Benjamin Disraeli, Benjamin Franklin, and John F. Kennedy), musicians (Bob Dylan and John Lennon), and poets (John Donne, Robert Frost, John Gay, Alfred Tennyson, and Ralph Waldo Emerson). The topics range from the sublime (Herman Melville's *Moby Dick*) to the absurd (Lewis Carroll's *Alice in Wonderland*).

This is not a book of famous legal quotations, such as "one person, one vote" or "separate but equal." Instead, this is a book of quotations, from unusual and thought-provoking non-judicial sources, where the quotations crystallize an important issue being debated before the Supreme Court.

Each quotation is properly cited and followed by a summary of how it was used in the underlying case. The sequence is deliberate: by offering the quote first, the reader is invited to wonder why the Justice selected it. The summary provides the answer.

The topics blend contemporary culture with scholarly ideas. By gathering the most interesting quotes as selected by the Justices themselves, *Supreme Quotes* appeals to those with even a casual interest in legal issues. It also offers an approachable method to learn about complex subjects because each quote illustrates the nub of the controversy.

Although the quotations are easily accessible, every case involves a matter of great public importance. For example, Justice Brennan quoted George Orwell's *Nineteen Eighty-Four* as part of his dissent in *Florida v. Riley*, an important search and seizure case. Similarly, Justice Stewart quoted Joseph Heller's *Catch-22* in *Parker v. Levy*, a court-martial case arising out of opposition to the Vietnam War. Likewise, Chief Justice

Rehnquist quoted Shakespeare's Othello in *Milkovich v. Lorain Journal Co.*, one of the Court's most important defamation cases.

Occasionally, the quotation reveals something personal about the Justice. For example, Justice Souter, who retired to New Hampshire, quoted Robert Frost, the poet most identified with that State. Virgil's *Aeneid* was quoted by Justice Field, which was reminiscent of his childhood trip to the Greek Isles and Turkey, in the vicinity of the mythic city of Troy. Notably, Justice Ginsburg, who became somewhat of a pop culture sensation, quoted from two cult classics: *Alice in Wonderland* and the television series M*A*S*H. Shakespeare was quoted repeatedly by Justice Rehnquist, who was known for making cameo appearances at the local Shakespeare Theater (Elaine Sciolino, "Lear Gets a Break from Supreme Court Justices Who Think the Play's the Thing," *N.Y. Times*, June 16, 2001).

Overall, if you enjoy thought-provoking quotations that provide insight about matters of great public interest, then you will enjoy *Supreme Quotes*.

Franklin Pierce Adams, 1913 (photograph by Harris & Ewing)

FRANKLIN PIERCE ADAMS

These are the saddest of possible words,
"Tinker to Evers to Chance."
Trio of bear cubs, and fleeter than birds,
"Tinker to Evers to Chance."
Ruthlessly pricking our gonfalon bubble,
Making a Giant hit into a double—
Words that are weighty with nothing but trouble:
"Tinker to Evers to Chance."

Flood v. Kuhn, 407 U.S. 258, 264 n.5 (1972) (Blackmun, J.) (quoting Franklin Pierce Adams, "Baseball's Sad Lexicon").

In 1969, the St. Louis Cardinals traded center fielder Curt Flood to the Philadelphia Phillies. At the time, Flood was the Cardinals' co-captain, a seven-time Gold Glove award winner, and a major contributor to the Cardinals' World Series victories in 1964 and 1967. Nevertheless, like all professional baseball players at the time, Flood had no right to refuse the trade because he was subject to the so-called "reserve system" which, since 1887, empowered baseball teams to trade their players at will.

Flood challenged the system by filing an antitrust action against Commissioner Bowie Kuhn and all the major league teams. The Supreme Court, however, rejected Flood's claim based on the unique and longstanding antitrust exemption that applied to Major League Baseball.

Writing for the majority, Justice Blackmun waxed eloquent about America's national pastime, including the lines, quoted above, immortalizing the famous Chicago Cubs double-play combination of shortstop Joe Tinker, second baseman Johnny Evers, and first baseman Frank Chance. *New York Times* columnist Franklin Pierce Adams wrote the poem to describe how his beloved New York Giants always lost to the Cubs. As for Flood, he lost his lawsuit, but he is widely credited for starting the movement that resulted in Major League Baseball's eventual decision to eliminate the "reserve system."

Alan Alda, circa 1960s (photograph by Friedman-Abeles, New York)

ALAN ALDA

I will not carry a gun…. I'll carry your books, I'll carry a torch, I'll carry a tune, I'll carry on, carry over, carry forward, Cary Grant, cash and carry, carry me back to Old Virginia, I'll even 'hari-kari' if you show me how, but I will not carry a gun!

Muscarello v. United States, 524 U.S. 125, 144 n.6 (1998) (Ginsburg, J., dissenting) (quoting Alan Alda playing the role of Hawkeye Pierce in the television series "M*A*S*H").

It should come as no surprise that a drug dealer might keep a pistol in his glove compartment as he drives to the scene of a drug deal. When that happens, the drug dealer is subject to a five-year mandatory minimum prison term if the court rules that he "carries" a firearm in relation to the drug deal.

The applicable statute, however, did not define the word "carries," which inspired the majority of the Supreme Court to embark on a literary tour of that word's common usage, including examples found in the King James Bible ("[H]is servants carried him in a chariot to Jerusalem"), Daniel DeFoe's *Robinson Crusoe* ("[w]ith my boat, I carry'd away every Thing"), and Herman Melville's *Moby Dick* (the owners of Queequeg's ship "had lent him a [wheelbarrow], in which to carry his heavy chest to his boarding house").

Justice Ginsburg's dissent collected additional examples, including Charles Bronson in the movie *The Magnificent Seven* ("You think I am brave because I carry a gun; well, your fathers are much braver because they carry responsibility"), Rudyard Kipling ("There's a Legion that never was 'listed, That carries no colours or crest"), Theodore Roosevelt ("Speak softly and carry a big stick"), as well as the quote above from the television series. On balance, however, the majority's decision to impose a five-year mandatory minimum prison term carried the day.

*Humphrey Bogart, 1940 (photograph from Warner Brothers,
taken from the film* Brother Orchid*)*

HUMPHREY BOGART

Captain Louis Renault [Claude Rains]: What in heaven's name brought you to Casablanca?

Rick Blaine [Humphrey Bogart]: My health. I came to Casablanca for the waters.

Captain Renault: The waters? What waters? We're in the desert.

Rick Blaine: I was misinformed.

Rapanos v. United States, 547 U.S. 715, 727 n.2 (2006) (Scalia, J.) (quoting *Save Our Sonoran, Inc. v. Flowers*, 408 F.3d 1113, 1117 (9th Cir. 2005) (quoting the movie *Casablanca*, Warner Bros. 1942)).

In 1989, John Rapanos wanted to build a shopping center on his 230-acre Michigan property, so he backfilled the wetland areas. The water-saturated land was relatively distant from any significant waterway: it drained to the so-called Hoppler Drain, which ran to the Hoppler Creek, which flowed to the navigable Kawkalin River, which was 11 miles away.

When federal officials insisted Rapanos needed a Clean Water Act permit, he refused to apply. When federal inspectors attempted a site visit, Rapanos blocked them. When federal regulators issued "cease and desist" letters, Rapanos ignored them.

The federal government sued and asserted Clean Water Act jurisdiction on the grounds that Rapanos's wetlands fell within the statutory definition of "waters of the United States." The lower courts agreed and upheld Clean Water Act jurisdiction.

The Supreme Court vacated and remanded. In a plurality decision, Justice Scalia criticized the long history of lower court decisions upholding the federal government's "sweeping assertions of jurisdiction over ephemeral channels and drains." In one case—which Justice Scalia singled out as the "most implausibl[e] of all"—a court allowed federal enforcement over an arroyo in the middle of the desert where water only ran during "periods of heavy rain." For Justice Scalia, the absurdity of finding the "waters of the United States" in a desert was reminiscent of the famous *Casablanca* movie lines, quoted above.

Sir Thomas More, 1527 (painted by Hans Holbein the Younger)

ROBERT BOLT

Some men think the Earth is round, others think it flat;
it is a matter capable of question.
But if it is flat, will the King's command make it round?
And if it is round, will the King's command flatten it?
No, I will not sign.

Gibson v. Florida Legislative Investigation Committee, 372 U.S. 539, 574–75 (1963) (Douglas, J., concurring) (quoting Robert Bolt, *A Man for All Seasons* (1960), pp. 132–33).

Starting in 1956, the Florida legislature established a committee to investigate the National Association for the Advancement of Colored People (NAACP) for the ostensible purpose of weeding out communist sympathizers. When the legislative committee subpoenaed the membership list of the NAACP's Miami branch, the branch President appeared before the committee and announced his refusal to produce the list, which resulted in a finding of contempt, a six-month prison sentence, and a $1200 fine. The Supreme Court overturned the sanctions on the grounds the committee's tactics violated the NAACP's First Amendment right to freedom of association.

In a concurrence, Justice Douglas was so appalled by the committee's investigation that he compared it to the famous loyalty oath that Henry the Eighth demanded of Sir Thomas More, as immortalized in Robert Bolt's play, quoted above. According to Justice Douglas, the treatment of the NAACP, like the treatment of Sir Thomas More, was an "episode[ ] where men, harried and harassed by government, sought refuge in their conscience."

James Boswell of Auchinleck, diarist and biographer of Dr. Samuel Johnson, 1785 (portrait by Joshua Reynolds)

JAMES BOSWELL

Hell is paved with good intentions.

Burgett v. Texas, 389 U.S. 109, 117 n.2 (1967) (Warren, C.J., concurring) (quoting James Boswell, *The Life of Samuel Johnson* 257 (Great Books ed. 1952)).

In 1965, in Hunt County, Texas, James Cleveland Burgett was indicted for assault with intent to murder. Pursuant to a Texas "three strikes" statute, life imprisonment was required if the prosecution also proved the defendant had two prior felony convictions.

The indictment, which was read in its entirety to the jury, listed four prior convictions, but the prosecution failed to prove any of them. For one of the convictions, the proof was facially void and excluded from evidence. For two of the convictions, the prosecution failed to offer any proof. And for the last conviction, the proof reflected the appellant had not been represented by counsel.

Of all the flaws, the Supreme Court seized on the last because it was contrary to *Gideon v. Wainright*, which established a Constitutional right to counsel in criminal cases. In a 6-3 decision, the Court reversed Burgett's conviction in part because the jury heard evidence of that tainted criminal conviction, and it was unrealistic to expect the jury to disregard the evidence, even though the trial judge instructed them to do so.

Justice Harlan dissented and argued for a "good faith" exception. Chief Justice Warren disagreed and insisted the case should not turn on the "prosecutor's good or bad faith." Instead, Chief Justice Warren quipped that, if the defendant's conviction were allowed to stand, then the defendant's "road to prison" would be paved with the same good intentions as Samuel Johnson's proverbial "road to hell," as articulated in James Boswell's classic biography.

Albert Camus, pre-1958 (unknown photographer)

ALBERT CAMUS

The man who enjoys his coffee while reading that justice has been done would spit it out at the least detail.

Glass v. Louisiana, 471 U.S. 1080, 1087 n.12 (1985) (Brennan, J., dissenting) (quoting Albert Camus, "Reflections on the Guillotine," *Resistance, Rebellion, and Death* 187 (1961)).

In 1982, Jimmy Glass and Jimmy Wingo escaped from a Louisiana jail, broke into a private home, and held a husband and wife at gunpoint. After ransacking the house, Wingo decided the couple had to be killed because they heard Glass mention Wingo's name. Under threats from Wingo, Glass murdered the couple at point blank range. Both Wingo and Glass were convicted and sentenced to death by electrocution. Glass requested Supreme Court review, but a majority declined to hear the case.

In a dissent, Justice Brennan explained he would have granted review and ruled that electrocution was unconstitutional "cruel and unusual punishment." In support of his argument, Justice Brennan offered a gruesome detailed description of the mechanics of an electrocution, including how it sometimes would cause the condemned man's eyeballs to "pop out." Justice Brennan surmised that, if the public were aware of such details, it would trigger the kind of reaction described above, in the quote from the French existentialist writer.

George Carlin, 1975 (publicity photo, Little David Records)

GEORGE CARLIN

I was thinking one night about the words you couldn't say on the public ... airwaves, ... the ones you definitely wouldn't say, ever ... and it came down to seven but the list is open to amendment....

Federal Communications Commission v. Pacifica Foundation, 438 U.S. 726, 751–52 (1978) (Appendix to Opinion of the Court) (quoting "Filthy Words," George Carlin's stand-up comedy routine).

Perhaps the most vulgar language ever published as part of a Supreme Court decision—words that will not be reproduced here—may be found in the Appendix to the Court's opinion in *Federal Communications Commission v. Pacifica Foundation*, which includes a verbatim transcript of George Carlin's 1973 live performance of his famous comedy routine, "Filthy Words."

In *Pacifica*, the FCC sanctioned a New York radio station for broadcasting Carlin's monologue during a time of day when it might have been heard by children. The Court issued a narrow ruling upholding the FCC's sanction on nuisance grounds, while avoiding a decision about whether Carlin's language was obscene. On the latter issue, Justice Brennan's dissent quoted a variety of off-color Bible passages to illustrate, in essence, that obscenity in one context may not be obscenity in another.

.I.

The White Rabbit, 1890 (Image taken from The Nursery Alice,
originally published by Macmillan & Co., London)

LEWIS CARROLL

"Herald, read the accusation!" said the King.

On this the White Rabbit blew three blasts on the trumpet, and then unrolled the parchment scroll, and read as follows: "The Queen of Hearts, she made some tarts, all on a summer day: The Knave of Hearts, he stole those tarts, and took them quite away!"

"Consider your verdict," the King said to the jury.

"Not yet, not yet!" the Rabbit interrupted. "There's a great deal to come before that!"

Nelson v. Adams USA, Inc., 529 U.S. 460, 468 n.2 (2000) (Ginsburg, J.) (quoting Lewis Carroll, *Alice in Wonderland and Through the Looking Glass* 108 (Messner 1982)).

Procedural unfairness was Justice Ginsburg's theme when she wrote for a unanimous court in *Nelson*. The case involved a judgment against a corporation that appeared uncollectible, which caused the plaintiff to request an unusual post-judgment amendment: a request that the corporation's president not only be added as a party, but also that the judgment be amended to make the corporation's president personally financially responsible.

The trial court granted the unusual request, but the Supreme Court reversed, due to the unfairness of the corporation's president being "adjudged liable the very first moment his personal liability was legally at issue."

The Dalai Lama (Tenzin Gyatso) at Boston, October 2012
(photograph by Christopher Michel)

THE DALAI LAMA

I am a Buddhist monk—a simple Buddhist monk—so we pray to
Buddha and all other Gods….

Town of Greece v. Galloway, 572 U.S. 565, 579 (2014) (Kennedy, J.)
(quoting the Dalai Lama's March 6, 2014 opening prayer to the U.S.
Congress, as reported in 160 Cong. Rec. S1329).

In 1999, the Town of Greece, in upstate New York, decided to invite
local clergy to begin each Board meeting with a prayer. In order to find
volunteer chaplains, the Town used the Chamber of Commerce's
Community Guide, which listed the local houses of worship, all of which
happened to be Christian. Considering the pool from which the Town was
drawing, it was no surprise that all of the volunteer chaplains were
Christian. Moreover, some of the prayers utilized overtly Christian themes,
including references to "our brother Jesus," and the "sacrifice of Jesus
Christ on the cross."

In 2008, Susan Galloway and Linda Staples attended a Board meeting,
and they were offended by the overt religiosity. In response to their com-
plaints, the Town arranged for prayers from a Jewish layman, as well as the
chairman of the local Baha'i temple. When a Wiccan priestess learned of
the controversy, she asked for permission to provide a prayer, and the Town
agreed. Nevertheless, Galloway and Staples sought a federal injunction to
limit the prayers to those that were inclusive and respectful of all faiths. The
District Court granted summary judgment in favor of the Town. The U.S.
Court of Appeals for the Second Circuit reversed and ruled for Galloway
and Staples. The Supreme Court reversed and ruled for the Town.

Justice Kagan's dissent asserted the Town's prayers violated the First
Amendment. As Justice Kagan put it, the Establishment Clause was meant
to ensure that government institutions belong "no less to the Buddhist or
Hindu than to the Methodist or Episcopalian." For rhetorical support,
Justice Kagan recalled George Washington's 1790 visit to Newport, Rhode
Island, the site of America's first Jewish community, where our first
President wrote eloquently regarding equality of citizenship, regardless of
religion.

The majority, however, was more interested in favorably comparing
the Town's prayers to those used to open each session of the United States
Congress. Writing for the majority, Justice Kennedy quoted several Congressional prayers, including those from Muslim leader Nayyar Imam ("The

final prophet of God, Muhammad, peace be upon him, stated: 'The leaders of a people are a representation of their deeds'"), Hindu monk Satguru Bodhinatha Veylanswami ("Hindu scripture declares, without equivocation, that the highest of high ideals is to never knowingly harm anyone"), and Rabbi Joshua Gruenberg ("Our God and God of our ancestors, Everlasting Spirit of the Universe..."). Finally, Justice Kennedy offered a Congressional prayer from his Holiness, the Dalai Lama, as quoted above, the text of which, ironically, reflected exactly the kind of religious inclusiveness that undoubtedly would have satisfied Galloway and Staples.

Clarence Darrow, attorney, 1922 (photograph by Herzog, Rockford, Ill.)

CLARENCE DARROW

I do not know how much salvage there is in these two boys... [Y]our Honor would be merciful if you tied a rope around their necks and let them die; merciful to them, but not merciful to civilization, and not merciful to those who would be left behind.

Yarborough v. Gentry, 540 U.S. 1, 10 (2003) (*per curiam*) (quoting Clarence Darrow's closing argument in the Leopold and Loeb murder case, as reported in *Famous American Jury Speeches* 1086) (F. Hicks ed. 1925) (reprint 1990)).

In *Yarborough*, a criminal defense attorney delivered a closing argument in which he described his own client as a "lousy drug addict," a "stinking thief," and a "jail bird." The question before the Supreme Court was whether the closing argument was so substandard that it violated the client's constitutional right to a fair trial.

In a unanimous decision, the Supreme Court said no. On the contrary, the Justices surmised the criminal defense attorney might have been disparaging his own client in order to elicit sympathy and gain a tactical advantage that was similar to the way Clarence Darrow successfully defended his clients in the famous Leopold and Loeb murder case, quoted above.

BENJ. DISRAELI, EARL OF BEACONSFIELD.

Benjamin Disraeli, British Prime Minister (from John Clark Ridpath et al.,
Life and Work of James G. Blaine, *1893)*

BENJAMIN DISRAELI

There are three kinds of lies: lies, damned lies, and statistics.

Procter & Gamble Mfg. Co. v. Fisher, 449 U.S. 1115, 1118 (1981)
(Rehnquist, J., dissenting) (quoting nineteenth century British Prime Minister Benjamin Disraeli).

In 1974, a class action lawsuit was filed against Procter & Gamble by Black employees who alleged the company's promotion system had a racially discriminatory disparate impact. The suit relied heavily on statistical evidence, which showed black employees were over-represented among the company's "lower echelon." After a bench trial, the District Court found the company liable, the U.S. Court of Appeals for the Fifth Circuit affirmed, and the Supreme Court denied the company's petition for a writ of certiorari.

In his dissent, Justice Rehnquist was appalled by the loose use of statistical evidence. Indeed, Justice Rehnquist had little trouble pointing out how the same statistics could lead to the opposite conclusion. For example, Justice Rehnquist noted the failure to consider that the company's recent affirmative action program may have been so successful it resulted in more entry-level minority employees, who by definition are in the "lower echelon." On the flip side, Justice Rehnquist explained the lack of more "higher echelon" minority employees could have been the result of the company's legitimate promotions based on seniority, not race. Expressing his disdain, Justice Rehnquist offered nineteenth century British Prime Minister Benjamin Disraeli's familiar observation, quoted above.

John Donne, circa 1622, English poet and cleric (portrait by Isaac Oliver)

JOHN DONNE

No man is an island.

Sierra Club v. Morton, 405 U.S. 727, 760, n.2 (1972) (Blackmun, J., dissenting) (quoting John Donne, *Devotions* XVII).

In 1969, Walt Disney Enterprises obtained government approval to build a $35 million ski resort at Mineral King Valley in California's Sierra Nevada Mountains. To provide access to the resort, the U.S. Department of the Interior approved the construction of a 20-mile highway, and a high-voltage power line, which would traverse nearby Sequoia National Park.

In an effort to block the development, the Sierra Club sought Administrative Procedure Act judicial review on the grounds the Department of Interior's approval violated various statutes and regulations. The Sierra Club sued as an organization with a "special interest" in the conservation and maintenance of national parks, but none of the named plaintiffs alleged they used the park or would be personally affected by the proposed resort, road, and utility lines.

In the absence of a "personal stake" in the controversy, the Supreme Court concluded the plaintiffs lacked standing to sue as "representatives of the public." Writing for the majority, Justice Stewart quoted *Democracy in America*, written in the 1830s by Alex de Tocqueville, who warned that judicial review should only be available to remedy a concrete injury, as opposed to a partisan faction's generalized grievance.

Justice Blackmun dissented because this was no ordinary litigation, but rather an example of the "world's deteriorating environment" due to "ecological disturbances." For such cases, Justice Blackmun would have allowed "an imaginative expansion" of traditional standing concepts to allow well-recognized groups, like the Sierra Club, to litigate on behalf of the public interest. As for the majority's reliance on de Tocqueville regarding whether the Sierra Club had a "personal stake" in the controversy, Justice Blackmun insisted that, at least in the environmental context, he would personally prefer John Donne's older and more pertinent observation, quoted above.

Arthur Conan Doyle, 1914 (from Current History of the War v.I.
New York Times Co.)

ARTHUR CONAN DOYLE

The dog that did not bark.

Chisom v. Roemer, 501 U.S. 380, 396 n.23 (1991) (Stevens, J.) (citing Arthur Conan Doyle, Silver Blaze, in *The Complete Sherlock Holmes* 335 (1927)).

When Congress passed the Voting Rights Act of 1965, it applied to the election of politicians and judges. In 1982, Congress expanded the Act to prohibit practices that inhibited the right to vote, regardless of discriminatory intent. However, the 1982 legislation used the term "representatives," which suggested the expanded Voting Rights Act only applied to the election of politicians (who "represent" voters) as opposed to judges (who do not).

In 1986, a class of 135,000 black registered voters in Orleans Parish, Louisiana, challenged their local judicial election system. The District Court dismissed the case because it concluded judges were not "representatives." The decision was reversed by a three-judge panel of the U.S. Court of Appeals for the Fifth Circuit. But after a remand, and in a related case, the entire Fifth Circuit returned to the District Court's reasoning and concluded the expanded Voting Rights Act did not apply to judicial elections.

The Supreme Court disagreed. Writing for the majority, Justice Stevens insisted that, when expanding the Voting Rights Act, if Congress had intended to exclude judicial elections, then "Congress would have made it explicit in the statute," or Congress would have mentioned it in the legislative history. For support, Justice Stevens relied on the Sherlock Holmes story, "Silver Blaze," in which the famous detective solved the mystery because a dog did not bark.

Justice Scalia was unmoved. In dissent, he reminded his fellow Justices the Court had previously rejected "the Conan Doyle approach to statutory construction." *Chisom v. Roemer*, 501 U.S. 380, 406 (1991) (Scalia, J., dissenting) (citing *Harrison v. PPG Industries, Inc.*, 446 U.S. 578, 592 (1980) ("In ascertaining the meaning of a statute, a court cannot, in the manner of Sherlock Holmes, pursue the theory of the dog that did not bark"). Expanding on the canine metaphor, Justice Scalia emphasized the importance of applying the statutory text because, as he put it, "[s]tatutes are the law though sleeping dogs lie."

Bob Dylan, onstage in Victoria-Gasteiz at the Azkena Rock Festival,
2010 (photograph by Alberto Cabello)

BOB DYLAN

> When you got nothing, you got nothing to lose.

Sprint Communications, Co., L.P. v. APCC Services, Inc., 554 U.S. 269, 301 (2008) (Roberts, C.J., dissenting) (quoting Bob Dylan, "Like A Rolling Stone," on *Highway 61 Revisited* (Columbia Records 1965)).

Before cellphones became ubiquitous, there was a time when long distance calls were made on payphones using discount access cards from companies like Sprint. When that happened, Sprint was required to compensate the payphone operator. But since each individual transaction was so small, payphone operators assigned collection rights to companies called aggregators, who received a fee for their collection services, while handing over any recovery to the payphone operators.

In 2003, in response to an aggregator lawsuit, Sprint moved to dismiss on the grounds the aggregators lacked standing. The Supreme Court ruled 5-4 the aggregators had standing. Chief Justice Roberts dissented.

According to Chief Justice Roberts, standing should have been denied because the aggregators did not even have a "dollar or two" at stake in the litigation. His fear was that, if courts were to hear lawsuits by companies with no stake in the outcome, then lawsuits would be transformed into "a marketable commodity," assignable to anyone.

Considering the aggregators had "nothing to gain," and insisting there is a "legal difference between something and nothing," Chief Justice Roberts rolled out Bob Dylan's famous truism, quoted above.

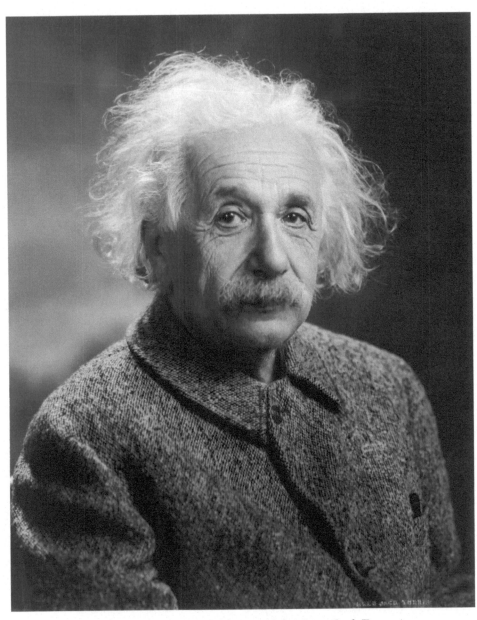

Albert Einstein, 1947 (photograph by Oren Jack Turner)

ALBERT EINSTEIN

... [P]eople understand one another with difficulty unless talking face to face.

Kleindienst v Mandel, 408 U.S. 53, 776 n.2 (1972) (Marshall, J., dissenting) (quoting Albert Einstein, as quoted in *Developments in the Law—The National Security Interest and Civil Liberties*, 85 Harv. L. Rev. 1130, 1154 (1972)).

In the 1960s, Ernest Mandel was the editor-in-chief of the Belgian Socialist weekly *La Gauche*. Mandel was a self-described "revolutionary Marxist" and a prominent advocate for world communism. By statute, however, anyone who advocated communism was prohibited from entering the United States, unless the Attorney General granted a discretionary visa.

In 1962, the Kennedy Administration's Attorney General (Robert F. Kennedy) authorized a visa, which allowed Mandel to enter the United States as a journalist. In 1968, the Johnson Administration's Attorney General (Ramsey Clark) authorized a second visa, which allowed Mandel to lecture at various American universities. In 1969, however, the Nixon Administration's Attorney General (John Mitchell) denied a third visa, which prohibited Mandel from entering the country to lecture at more American universities.

A lawsuit was filed by the American scholars who invited Mandel to speak. Those scholars insisted they had a First Amendment right to hear Mandel's lectures, and the government was interfering with free speech by denying Mandel's visa.

The Supreme Court disagreed. Writing for the majority, Justice Blackmun did not view the case through a First Amendment lens. Instead, he focused on the more tangible principle that the government has nearly unlimited authority to decide who may (and who may not) enter the country. Essentially, for Justice Blackmun, this was a dispute about permission to cross the border, not censorship.

In dissent, Justice Marshall saw it quite differently. From Justice Marshall's perspective, it made no difference whether Mandel's books and ideas were widely available. Instead, Justice Marshall insisted that, for First Amendment purposes, a visa should have been granted because there was no substitute for Mandel's in-person lectures. In support of the unique importance of face-to-face communication, Justice Marshall turned to Albert Einstein, as quoted above.

Ralph Waldo Emerson, American writer, circa 1857
(unknown photographer)

RALPH WALDO EMERSON

By the rude bridge that arched the flood
Their flag to April's breeze unfurled,
Here once the embattled farmers stood
And fired the shot heard 'round the world.

Texas v. Johnson, 491 U.S. 397, 422 (1989) (Rehnquist, C.J, dissenting) (quoting Ralph Waldo Emerson's "Concord Hymn").

In 1984, at the Republican National Convention in Dallas, Gregory Lee Johnson unfurled an American flag, doused it with kerosene, and set it on fire while protestors chanted: "America, the red, white, and blue, we spit on you." Charged with "desecration of a venerated object," in violation of the Texas Penal Code, Johnson was tried, convicted, fined, and sentenced to one year in prison.

In a 5-4 decision, the Supreme Court relied on the First Amendment to overturn Johnson's conviction. Writing for the majority, Justice Brennan concluded that Johnson had engaged in "expressive conduct," and that Johnson's conviction was not justified by the State's interest in preserving the flag as a symbol of national unity.

Writing for the dissent, Chief Justice Rehnquist argued the flag was not simply a "point of view," but rather a symbol so revered that its desecration had been criminalized by 48 States and the federal government. Chief Justice Rehnquist then offered a stars-and-stripes history lesson that included the War of 1812's inspiration for the Star Spangled Banner, the World War II flag-raising on Iowa Jima, and the soldiers who planted a flag in Korea after the heroic Inchon amphibious landing. The Chief Justice's history lesson began with Ralph Waldo Emerson's 1837 poem, "Concord Hymn," quoted above.

Anatole France, circa 1920 (photograph by Henri Manuel)

ANATOLE FRANCE

The law, in its majestic equality,
forbids the rich as well as the poor
to sleep under bridges, to beg in the streets, and to steal bread.

Reck v. Pate, 367 U.S. 433, 446 n.5 (1961) (Douglas, J., concurring) (quoting Anatole France, as quoted in Cournos, *A Modern Plutarch* (1928), p. 27).

In 1961, the Supreme Court reversed Emil Reck's murder conviction because it was based on a coerced confession. The coercion included several days of police interrogation without allowing Reck to communicate with his father, a lawyer, a judge, or even doctors (sent by the prosecutor's office) to determine if Reck was being beaten by the police.

Justice Douglas wrote separately to emphasize that totalitarian regimes similarly extract confessions by holding prisoners "incommunicado." According to Justice Douglas, many Communist countries considered it "the secret of successful interrogation." From Justice Douglas's perspective, preventing the accused from speaking with the outside world was reminiscent of the Spanish Inquisition.

Turning to American law enforcement, Justice Douglas bemoaned how the police use the same technique to extract confessions from those, like Reck, of "lowly birth," who lack "friends or status." To illustrate the unfair treatment of the poor and the powerless, Justice Douglas quoted poet and novelist Anatole France.

Benjamin Franklin, 1826 (lithograph by J. B. Mauzaisse)

BENJAMIN FRANKLIN

> In this world nothing can be said to be certain, except death and taxes.

United States v. Estate of Romani, 523 U.S. 517, 520 n.2 (1988) (Stevens, J.) (quoting Benjamin Franklin's November 13, 1789 letter to Jean Baptiste LeRoy, as published in 10 *The Writings of Benjamin Franklin* 69 (A. Smyth ed. 1907)).

In 1985, a private creditor recorded a $400,000 judgment lien against Francis Romani's Pennsylvania real estate. Soon thereafter, the federal government recorded $490,000 in tax liens against the same property. All of the debts remained uncollected until 1992, when Romani died, and his real estate was valued at only $53,000.

The shortfall triggered a $53,000 collection dispute between the private creditor and the federal government. The central issue involved an inconsistency between two federal statutes. One was the federal priority statute, 31 U.S.C. § 3713, which provided the federal government "shall be paid first" when a decedent's estate cannot pay all of its debts. The other was the Federal Tax Lien Act, 26 U.S.C. § 6321, which declared that a federal tax lien "shall not be valid" against a previously recorded judgment lien.

The federal government's attempt to rely on the first statute, while ignoring the second, raised the ire of Justice Stevens, who opined that the government's aggressive collection tactics "gave new meaning to Franklin's aphorism," quoted above. Writing for the unanimous Court, Justice Stevens concluded the Federal Tax Lien Act blocked the government's collection efforts, thus proving that while death is inevitable, taxes are not.

Ivy-covered wall (photograph by Sergey Okhrymenko)

ROBERT FROST

Before I built a wall I'd ask to know what I was walling in or
walling out.

Plaut v. Spendthrift Farm, Inc., 514 U.S. 211, 245 (1995) (Breyer, J.,
concurring) (quoting Robert Frost, "Mending Wall," *The New Oxford Book
of American Verse* 395–96 (R. Ellmann ed. 1976)).

In *Spendthrift Farm*, the Supreme Court considered the constitution-
ality of a law that would have revived certain securities fraud cases that had
been dismissed due to the expiration of the statute of limitations. The
Supreme Court concluded that the law violated "separation of powers"
because it involved a Congressional mandate for federal courts to set aside
previously issued final judgments. Writing for the majority, Justice Scalia
emphasized the importance of "separation of powers," by analogizing to the
idea that "good fences make good neighbors."

In response, Justice Breyer pointed out the phrase comes from the
Robert Frost poem "Mending Wall," which actually used the concept
ironically to suggest that some walls might best be torn down. Relying on a
different passage from the same Frost poem, Justice Breyer explained that
the value of a fence, like the value of "separation of powers," depends on
what you are "walling in or walling out."

Robert Frost, poet-farmer, 1941 (World-Telegram
photograph by Fred Palumbo)

ROBERT FROST

My object of living is "to unite [m]y avocation and my vocation."

Garcetti v. Ceballos, 547 U.S. 410, 432 at n.3 (2006) (Souter, J., dissenting) (quoting Robert Frost, Two Tramps in Mud Time, *Collected Poems, Prose & Plays* 251, 252 (R. Poirier & M. Richardson eds. 1995)).

When a government employee speaks out on a matter of public interest, does the First Amendment protect that speech? Or is the government allowed to impose discipline if it is unhappy with the content?

The answer is: it depends.

Prior to *Garcetti v. Ceballos*, in the context of teachers who spoke out about various public issues, the Supreme Court seemed to be expanding First Amendment protection. In one case, *Pickering v. Board of Education*, 391 U.S. 563 (1968), the Court concluded the First Amendment protected a teacher who wrote a letter to her local newspaper about a school funding issue. In another case, *Givhan v. Western Line Consolidated School District*, 439 U.S. 410 (1979), the Court likewise found the First Amendment protected a teacher who complained to her principal about racial hiring practices.

But in *Garcetti v. Ceballos*, the Supreme Court took a different approach. Writing for a 5-4 majority, Justice Kennedy concluded the First Amendment did not protect communications in the course of official duties. Specifically, in *Garcetti*, the government was allowed to discipline Los Angeles County Deputy District Attorney Richard Ceballos, who wrote a controversial memo to his supervisors regarding his belief there were misrepresentations in a search warrant affidavit.

For Justice Kennedy, the key distinction was that the First Amendment protected the teachers in *Pickering* and *Givhan* because they were commenting in their personal capacities about topics that were outside their job descriptions (hiring practices and school funding). In contrast, in *Garcetti*, there was no First Amendment protection because Ceballos wrote his memo in his official capacity overseeing the reliability of search warrant affidavits.

In *Garcetti*, Justice Souter dissented because, perhaps, Ceballos was speaking in both capacities at the same time. In support of that duality, Justice Souter relied on the Robert Frost poem, quoted above, about how some seek to unite their avocation with their vocation.

The poem was clearly a Souter favorite because he quoted it again upon his 2009 retirement from the Court (Adam Liptak, "Poetry, as Souter

Takes Leave," *New York Times*, June 29, 2009). Indeed, at the retirement party, the other Justices celebrated Souter's decision to retire to New Hampshire's land of "easy wind and downy flake," a phrase they borrowed from another Robert Frost poem, "Stopping by Woods on a Snowy Evening."

Clark Gable, circa 1940 (publicity photo, movie studio)

CLARK GABLE

Frankly, my dear, I don't give a damn.

Bethel School District Number 403 v. Fraser, 478 U.S. 675, 691 (1986) (Stevens, J., dissenting) (quoting Clark Gable, as Rhett Butler, in the 1939 film *Gone with the Wind*).

In the State of Washington, a Bethel High School student nominated a friend for student council with a speech laced with sophomoric sexual innuendo, such as: "I know a man who is firm—he's firm in his pants, he's firm in his shirt, his character is firm—but most ... of all, his belief in you, the students of Bethel, is firm." Based on a school disciplinary rule that prohibited the use of "obscene, profane language or gestures," the school suspended the student for three days and prohibited him from participating as a graduation speaker.

The Supreme Court upheld the school's authority to impose the discipline, but the Justices split over the implications for free speech in a school setting. In a dissenting opinion, Justice Stevens used the Clark Gable quote to illustrate how some speech may be shocking to one generation but benign to another. As Justice Stevens explained, "[w]hen I was a high school student, the use of those words in a public forum shocked the Nation."

John Gay, pre-1732 (From a sketch by Sir Godfrey Kneller)

JOHN GAY

An open foe may prove a curse, but a pretended friend is worse.

Spano v. People of the State of New York, 360 U.S. 315, 323 (1959) (Warren, C.J.) (quoting 18th century English poet and dramatist John Gay).

On January 22, 1957, outside a Bronx bar, Vincent Joseph Spano got into a fight with a former professional boxer. Spano was knocked down and kicked in the head several times. After the fight, Spano walked to his apartment, grabbed a gun, and used the gun to shoot and kill the former boxer. Spano went into hiding, but on February 1st, he was indicted by a grand jury.

On February 3rd, Spano phoned his close friend, Gaspar Bruno, a fledgling police officer who had not yet finished police academy training. On the phone, Spano admitted he was the shooter, but he told Bruno that he was so dazed from the fight that he didn't know what he was doing.

On February 4th, Spano surrendered himself to the District Attorney. Spano's lawyer had cautioned him not to answer any questions, and Spano initially followed those instructions. Moreover, during questioning, Spano repeatedly requested to speak with his lawyer, but his requests were all denied.

Eventually, law enforcement decided to use Bruno, Spano's friend, in an effort to obtain a confession. The ploy was for Bruno to tell Spano that, as a result of the February 3rd phone call, Bruno was "in a lot of trouble" and he might lose his job, to the detriment of Bruno's pregnant wife and three children. After hearing Bruno's fictitious tale of woe, Spano decided to confess. And based on that confession, Spano was convicted by a jury and sentenced to death.

The Supreme Court reversed Spano's conviction and sentence. Chief Justice Warren concluded that the post-indictment confession was involuntary and contrary to the Fourteenth Amendment. In particular, Chief Justice Warren criticized the use of Bruno to exploit a "bond of friendship" when he was the one person Spano could trust. Upon recounting the details of Bruno's betrayal, the Chief Justice speculated Spano "was apparently unaware of John Gay's famous couplet," quoted above.

Ira Gershwin, 1925 or earlier (first found published in
Time, *Vol 6, July 20, 1925)*

IRA GERSHWIN

Plenty of nothing.

Bank Markazi v. Peterson, 136 S. Ct. 1310, 1335 (2016) (Roberts, C.J., dissenting) (quoting Ira Gershwin & DuBose Heyward, *Porgy and Bess*: Libretto 28 (1958)).

A group of American victims of Iranian state-sponsored terrorism obtained United States judgments against Iran worth billions of dollars. The plaintiffs, however, were unable to collect. To remedy that situation, Congress passed the Iran Threat Reduction and Syria Human Rights Act of 2012.

The Act was unusual because it only applied to the financial assets identified in the plaintiffs' collection action pending in the U.S District Court for the Southern District of New York. The Act's sole purpose was to authorize those particular plaintiffs to collect against specified assets as long as the District Court made very limited findings of fact, including that Iran had an equitable interest in the assets, and that the assets were held by a financial firm doing business in the United States.

Bank Markazi, the holder of the financial assets, argued the Act violated separation of powers because Congress was, essentially, dictating the result of a pending collection action. The District Court rejected the Bank's argument. The U.S. Court of Appeals for the Second Circuit affirmed. The Supreme Court also affirmed and allowed the asset collection.

Writing for the majority, Justice Ginsburg insisted Congress did not dictate the result of the collection action because, as the District Court explained, there was "plenty" to litigate regarding the Act's required factual findings. In dissent, Chief Justice Roberts scoffed at that description, particularly since all of the important factual findings were well-established before the Act was passed. Channeling Ira Gershwin's famous lyric in *Porgy and Bess*, the Chief Justice insisted the majority's "plenty" was actually "plenty of nothing," and that, apparently, "nothing is plenty for the Court."

First edition cover of Catch-22

JOSEPH HELLER

We accuse you also of the commission of crimes and infractions
we don't even know about yet. Guilty or innocent?
I don't know, sir. How can I say if you don't tell me what they are?
How can we tell you if we don't know?

Parker v. Levy, 417 U.S. 733, 788 n.41 (1974) (Stewart, J., dissenting) (quoting Joseph Heller, *Catch-22*, p. 395 (Dell ed. 1970)).

In 1967, an Army doctor was court-martialed for failing to carry out his medical duties and for making several public statements about his opposition to the Vietnam War. The doctor's court-martial was based on the Uniform Code of Military Justice, which prohibits "conduct unbecoming an officer and a gentleman." The doctor challenged his court-martial by arguing the phrase "conduct unbecoming an officer and a gentleman" was unconstitutionally vague. The Supreme Court disagreed and upheld the court-martial.

In dissent, Justice Stewart agreed with the doctor that the phrase was too vague to be enforceable. To illustrate his point, Justice Stewart likened the situation to a "Catch-22" in which neither the accuser nor the accused could articulate the basis of the charge.

Heracles and his child Telephos (marble sculpture in the Louvre Museum
by an unknown artist; Roman copy of the AD 1st–2nd century after
a Greek original of the 4th century BC. found in Tivoli, Italy)

HERCULES

[Hercules] now set out to perform his fifth Labour,
and this time his task was to cleanse the stables of
Augeas in a single day.

Sakraida v. Ag Pro, Inc., 425 U.S. 273, 275 n.1 (1976) (Brennan, J.)
(quoting C. Witt, *Classic Mythology* 119–20 (1883)).

Not every Supreme Court case is glamorous. Indeed, sometimes, the subject is nothing more than cow dung removal.

In 1968, in El Paso, Texas, a company known as Ag Pro sued Bernard Sakraida for infringing a patent for "a water flush system to remove cow manure from the floor of a dairy barn." The District Court concluded the system was not patentable because it utilized elements that were "old in the dairy business." Simply put, Ag Pro's system released water from a storage tank to wash the manure down a sloped floor into drains.

The U.S. Court of Appeals for the Fifth Circuit reversed and concluded the patent was valid. While conceding the system did not involve a "complicated technical improvement," the Fifth Circuit nevertheless opined it used a "novel combination" to achieve a "synergistic result."

That argument, however, did not wash with the Supreme Court. Writing for the unanimous Court, Justice Brennan was unimpressed with a system in which the only "inventive feature" was an "abrupt release of water." As a result, Justice Brennan agreed with the District Court that the system was nothing special, particularly for those "skilled in the art."

As Justice Brennan pointed out, "[s]ystems using flowing water to clean animal wastes from barn floors have been familiar on dairy farms since ancient times." For an ancient example, Justice Brennan relied on the fable of Hercules cleaning the Stables of Augeas by re-directing a nearby river, so that water "streamed in at one end and streamed out at the other, carrying away all the dirt with it."

The Reichstag building seen from the west. Inscription translates to "For/To the German People", 2009 (photograph by Matthew Field)

ADOLPH HITLER

If people [object] that only a judicial procedure
could precisely weigh the measure of the guilt ...,
then ... I lodge my most solemn protest.
He who rises against Germany is a traitor to his country....

Jay v. Boyd, 351 U.S. 345, 369 n. 12 (1956) (Black, J., dissenting) (quoting Adolph Hitler's July 13, 1934 Reichstag speech, as quoted in 1 *Hitler's Speeches* (Baynes ed. 1942) 321–24)).

In Supreme Court decisions, comparisons to Adolph Hitler are generally ill-advised. But, in the case of *Jay v. Boyd*, Justice Black could not resist.

The case involved Cecil Reginald Jay, a British citizen, who entered the United States in 1921. Between 1935 and 1940, Jay was a member of the Communist Party. In 1952, the federal government deported Jay pursuant to a statute that authorized the deportation of any alien who, at any time after entering the United States, became a member of the Communist Party.

The central dispute involved the government's denial of Jay's petition for discretionary relief. By statute, the Attorney General was authorized, "in his discretion," to cancel any deportation. By regulation, the exercise of that discretionary authority could be based on undisclosed confidential information. Jay alleged the regulation violated Due Process because it denied him the right to notice and the opportunity to challenge the evidence against him.

The Supreme Court upheld the regulation. Writing for the majority, Justice Reed concluded the regulation was valid because Congress granted the Attorney General "unfettered discretion" to decide whether to cancel a deportation. As Justice Reed put it, the Attorney General's authority to cancel a deportation was an "act of grace," not a matter of right.

In dissent, Justice Black was in no mood for grace. Instead, he warned the government's use of undisclosed confidential information posed a "grave danger" to our constitutional system. Justice Black offered a comparison to the Russian purges of the 1930s when, under Joseph Stalin, pardons were never granted to those facing execution. Justice Black also compared the situation to the Reichstag speech, quoted above, when Adolph Hitler declared his own unfettered authority to circumvent legal procedures.

Homer (photograph taken of the marble bust of Homer in the British Museum; Roman copy of a lost Hellenistic original of the c. 2nd BC. From Baiae, Italy)

HOMER

Even so did we seize the fiery-pointed brand
and whirled it round in his eye,
and the blood flowed about the heated bar.

Brown v. Entertainment Merchants Association, 564 U.S. 786, 796 (2011) (Scalia, J.) (quoting *The Odyssey of Homer*, Book IX, p. 125 (S. Butcher & A. Lang transls. 1909)).

In 2005, California passed a law prohibiting the sale of violent video games to minors. The Supreme Court struck down the law as an unconstitutional infringement on free speech.

Writing for the majority, Justice Scalia determined the First Amendment's Free Speech Clause protected violent video games just as it protected "books, plays, and movies." From Justice Scalia's perspective, all those forms of expression were protected because they communicated "ideas" and utilized "familiar literary devices," such as "characters, dialogue, plot, and music."

Expanding on that theme, Justice Scalia also pointed out how children's books commonly depict violence. One of his examples was Snow White, in which the wicked queen was punished by making her dance in red hot slippers "till she fell dead on the floor." Another example was Cinderella, in which the evil stepsisters had their eyes "pecked out by doves." Justice Scalia also cited Hansel and Gretel, who killed their captor by "baking her in an oven." But Justice Scalia's most gruesome example was Homer's Odyssey, in which Odysseus used a heated stake to blind the Cyclops Polyphemus, as quoted above.

John F. Kennedy, in the Oval Office, 1963 (photograph by Cecil Stoughton)

JOHN F. KENNEDY

> ... the rights of man come not from the generosity of the state
> but from the hand of God.

Engel v. Vitale, 370 U.S. 421, 448 n.3 (1962) (Stewart, J., dissenting) (quoting John F. Kennedy's Inaugural Address, January 20, 1961).

In 1959, in New Hyde Park, New York, the parents of ten students sued the Union Free School's Board of Education to halt the daily recitation of the following official school prayer: "Almighty God, we acknowledge our dependence upon Thee, and we beg Thy blessings upon us, our parents, our teachers and our Country."

The school adopted the prayer to comply with the "Statement On Moral and Spiritual Training in the Schools," issued by the Board of Regents, a state government agency with broad scholastic oversight powers. The parents argued the daily prayer, instituted at the government's direction, violated the First Amendment's Establishment Clause.

The Supreme Court agreed. Writing for the majority, Justice Black concluded the prayer was "religious activity" because it was a daily classroom "invocation of God's blessing" and a "solemn avowal of divine faith." For such activity, Justice Stewart offered a blanket condemnation: "it is no part of the business of government to compose official prayers for any group of the American people to recite as a part of a religious program carried on by government."

Such absolutism inspired Justice Stewart, in his dissent, to offer a series of counter-examples. One example came from George Washington's inaugural address, in which our first President offered "fervent supplications" to the "Almighty Being who rules over this universe." Another example was the quotation above, from the inaugural address of John F. Kennedy, who was President at the time the Supreme Court issued its decision. Yet another example invoked the traditions of the Supreme Court, which notably begins each session with the Crier's famous announcement: "God save the United States and this Honorable Court."

John Maynard Keynes, 1945 (unknown photographer)

JOHN MAYNARD KEYNES

In the long run we are all dead.

Tahoe-Sierra Preservation Council, Inc. v. Tahoe Regional Planning Agency, 535 U.S. 302, 356 (2002) (Thomas, J., dissenting) (quoting John Maynard Keynes, *Monetary Reform* 88 (1924)).

In the 1960s, in order to manage Lake Tahoe's development, California and Nevada created the Tahoe Regional Planning Agency. In 1980, while developing a new regional plan, the Agency limited the number of building permits and prohibited the development of new subdivisions, condominiums, and apartment buildings. In 1981, the Agency imposed a complete moratorium on development that was scheduled to last until the summer of 1982, which was the Agency's deadline to adopt a regional plan. As it became clear the Agency would miss the deadline, the moratorium was extended. In 1984, when the Agency finally adopted a plan, California enjoined implementation of the plan on the grounds it was not strict enough. While the injunction was in effect, the moratorium continued until a new plan was adopted in 1987.

For the Supreme Court, the issue was whether such a long moratorium was a Fifth Amendment taking. Writing for the majority, Justice Stevens concluded it was not. Noting the importance of protecting the unique environment around Lake Tahoe, Justice Stevens quoted Mark Twain, who famously described Lake Tahoe as a "noble sheet of blue water." As for the moratorium's economic impact, Justice Stevens concluded it was negligible because property values would eventually recover.

In dissent, Justice Thomas emphasized the moratorium's immediate economic harm, and he belittled the speculation about future property values. To illustrate the point, Justice Thomas quoted twentieth century British economist John Maynard Keynes, who pointedly described the folly of relying too much on what will happen "in the long run."

Stan Lee, at San Diego Comic Con, 1975 (photograph by Alan Light)

STAN LEE

[I]n this world, with great power there must also come—
great responsibility.

Kimble v. Marvel Entertainment, LLC, 576 U.S. 446, 465 (2015) (Kagan, J.) (quoting Stan Lee and Steve Ditko, Amazing Fantasy No. 15: "Spider-Man," p. 13 (1962)).

Kudos to Stephen Kimble who, in 1990, patented a Spider-Man toy, known as the "Web Blaster," which fits around the wrist, and shoots pressurized foam strings that are meant to look like superhero spider webs. Kimble licensed the rights to Marvel Entertainment in exchange for $500,000 plus an annual royalty payment.

Soon after the agreement, Marvel's lawyers devised a way to bring an end to those annual royalty payments. Marvel sought and obtained a declaratory judgment based on a lesser-known Supreme Court decision, *Brulotte v. Thys Co.*, 379 U.S. 29 (1964), in which the Justices announced a rule that, regardless of any contractual arrangements, royalty payments must cease upon the expiration of the underlying patent. For Kimble, 2010 was the patent expiration date.

When the case reached the Supreme Court, the debate involved *stare decisis*: the doctrine that legal precedents must be followed except in unusual circumstances. Justice Alito took the position that *Brulotte* was an unusual case that should be overturned because it imposed a wrongly decided judge-made rule that interfered with an inventor's right to earn income from his or her patent. The majority, however, reaffirmed *Brulotte* and ruled in favor of Marvel.

Writing for the majority, Justice Kagan emphasized the importance of exercising caution before overturning legal precedent. In support of her judicial restraint philosophy, Justice Kagan summoned the famous motto of the Web-Slinger's creators, as quoted above.

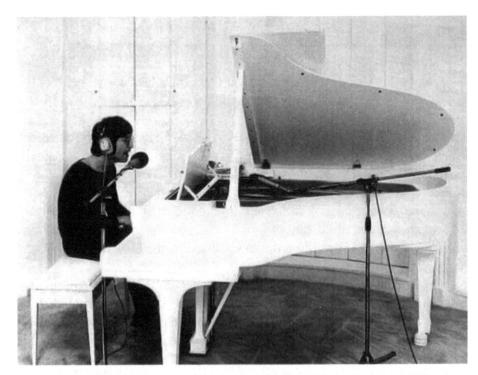

John Lennon, as pictured in an advertisement for Imagine *from* Billboard, *Sept. 18, 1971 (photograph by Peter Fordham)*

JOHN LENNON

Imagine there's no countries
It isn't hard to do
Nothing to kill or die for
And no religion too
Imagine all the people
Living life in peace.

Pleasant Grove City v. Summum, 555 U.S. 460, 475 n.2 (2009) (Alito, J.) (quoting John Lennon, "Imagine," on *Imagine* (Apple Records 1971)).

In 1971, the Fraternal Order of Eagles donated a Ten Commandments monument for permanent placement in Pioneer Park, Pleasant Grove City, Utah. In 2003, and again in 2005, the Gnostic Christian organization Summum offered to place its own stone monument in the park, which would be similar to the Ten Commandments monument, but instead the inscription would be "the Seven Aphorisms of Summum." Pleasant Grove denied the requests. Summum sued and alleged Pleasant Gove violated the Free Speech Clause by accepting a Ten Commandments monument while rejecting one for the Seven Aphorisms. A unanimous Supreme Court ruled for Pleasant Grove.

The central issue was whether a donated permanent monument in a public park was "private speech," which is subject to the Free Speech Clause, or "government speech," which is not. Writing for the Court, Justice Alito explained that when a government accepts a permanent monument (even one donated by a private citizen), it is "government speech," so the Free Speech Clause does not apply.

In such circumstances, to avoid the "government speech" doctrine from being used as a "subterfuge" to favor certain private speech, Summum argued that governments should be required to state, explicitly, the "message" they are promoting. The Court rejected the idea because of the difficulty of knowing a monument's true "message."

In support of that determination, Justice Alito relied on the New York Central Park's John Lennon monument, which states simply: "Imagine." According to Justice Alito, the "message" for some might be to "imagine" the musical contributions lost when Lennon was murdered, while for others the "message" would be the lyrics of Lennon's famous ballad, quoted above.

John McCrae, circa 1912 (unknown photographer)

JOHN MCCRAE

In Flanders fields the poppies blow
Between the crosses, row on row.

American Legion v. American Humanist Association, 139 S. Ct. 2067, 2075–76 (2019) (Alito, J.) (quoting John McCrae's poem in *Flanders Fields and Other Poems* 3 (G.P. Putnam's Sons ed. 1919)).

In 1925, private citizens built the Bladensburg cross to honor the Maryland soldiers who died in World War I. Also known as the Peace Cross, the monument was a 32-foot tall Latin cross, on a large pedestal, located within a traffic island at the center of a busy three-way intersection in Bladensburg, Maryland.

In 1961, the Bladensburg Cross was acquired by the Maryland-National Capital Park and Planning Commission, which is an agency of the State of Maryland. In 1985, the site was re-dedicated to honor local soldiers who died in all wars.

Litigation began in 2012, when the American Humanist Association alleged it violated the First Amendment's Establishment Clause for the Bladensburg cross to be maintained by public funds on public land. The U.S. District Court for the District of Maryland denied the claim based, in part, on the valid non-religious governmental purpose of honoring military sacrifices. The U.S. Court of Appeals for the Fourth Circuit reversed based, in part, on the inherent religious meaning of Christianity's preeminent symbol.

When the case reached the Supreme Court, similar intellectual battle lines were drawn. On one side was Justice Ginsburg, who insisted the display of the Latin cross on government property suggested government endorsement of that religious symbol. On the other side was Justice Thomas, who acknowledged the overt religious symbolism, while arguing it was not prohibited by the Constitution.

Justice Alito, however, was able to garner a plurality of support by emphasizing how, depending on the historical context, even a religious symbol like the Latin cross may have a non-religious meaning. One example was the use of the Latin cross as the widely-recognized symbol of the International Committee for the Red Cross. Another example was Blue Cross Blue Shield, which incorporated the Latin cross into its registered corporate trademark.

Turning to the world of history and poetry, Justice Alito explained how the use of the Latin cross could likewise be considered secular. For support, he invoked John McCrae's famous poem, quoted above, which used the imagery of the Latin cross to immortalize the World War I soldiers who died in Belgium along the infamous Western Front.

Illustration of the final chase of Moby-Dick (illustration by I.W. Taber in Moby Dick, *Charles Scribner's Sons, New York, 1902)*

HERMAN MELVILLE

Whether Leviathan can long endure so wide a chase,
and so remorseless a havoc;
whether he must not at last be exterminated from the waters,
and the last whale, like the last man, smoke his last pipe,
and then himself evaporate in the final puff.

Japan Whaling Association v. American Cetacean Society, 478 U.S. 221, 249–50 (1986) (Marshall, J., dissenting) (quoting Herman Melville, *Moby Dick* 436 (Signet ed. 1961)).

The United States and Japan signed a treaty that imposed quotas on whale hunting, but there was no penalty for non-compliance. To remedy that omission, Congress passed a law that would have required the United States government to impose sanctions if the Secretary of Commerce certified that Japan's fishing operations "diminished the effectiveness" of the treaty's whale hunting quotas. In an effort to avoid the Congressional mandate, the Executive Branch entered into a side deal that would have allowed Japan to ignore the whale hunting quotas in the short term as long as Japan promised to make a good faith effort to comply in the future.

Environmental groups sued to require the Secretary of Commerce to make the necessary certification and impose the mandatory sanctions. When the Supreme Court ruled against the environmental groups, Justice Marshall dissented and speculated whether the world's whale population "can long endure so wide a chase."

Portrait of Jesus Christ (unknown artist)

THE NEW TESTAMENT: ACTS

Now as he journeyed he approached Damascus, and suddenly a light from heaven flashed about him. And he fell to the ground and heard a voice saying to him, "Saul, Saul, why do you persecute me?" And he said, "Who are you, Lord?" and he said, "I am Jesus, whom you are persecuting; but rise and enter the city, and you will be told what you are to do."

Ehlert v. United States, 402 U.S. 99, 108 & n.2 (1971) (Douglas, J., dissenting) (quoting the New Testament, 9 Acts 3–6 (rev. Standard ed. 1952)).

On June 14, 1964, during the Vietnam War, William Ward Ehlert was drafted and ordered to report for induction. According to Ehlert, the receipt of the induction order crystallized his anti-war views, which he had not previously expressed. Ehlert asked his local draft board to reclassify him as a conscientious objector, but the governing regulations prohibited a last-minute change in status unless necessary due to circumstances "over which the registrant had no control." In Ehlert's case, the local draft board concluded his epiphany, upon being drafted, did not qualify as a matter beyond Ehlert's control. When Ehlert refused to serve in the military, he was prosecuted and convicted.

Ehlert challenged the reasonableness of the regulations, but the Supreme Court ruled against him. Writing for the majority, Justice Stewart deferred to the government's regulatory interpretation that would allow for a limited number of last-minute changes of heart, but only if due to "extraneous" events that were "objectively identifiable" and beyond the registrant's control.

Justice Douglas dissented and insisted the majority's view was "belied by experience" because, upon receipt of an induction order, a person might reasonably experience a dramatic and uncontrollable conversion and realize that he was a conscientious objector. To illustrate the point, Justice Douglas relied on the Bible passage, quoted above, about Saul of Tarsus, who was miraculously converted from Christian persecutor to Apostle, while traveling along the proverbial "road to Damascus."

Sioux Indians at the 1904 World's Fair (unknown photographer)

THE NEW TESTAMENT: MATTHEW

Judge not, that ye be not judged.

United States v. Sioux Nation of Indians, 448 U.S. 371, 437 (1980) (Rehnquist, J., dissenting) (quoting Matthew 7:1–3, King James version).

For more than a century, the Sioux Nation claimed the United States had unlawfully abrogated the Fort Laramie Treaty of 1868, in which the United States "solemnly agree[d]" that no unauthorized person "shall ever be permitted to pass over, settle upon, or reside" in the territory of the Great Sioux Reservation in South Dakota's Black Hills. In 1874, the government's "solemn" promise began to unravel when Lieutenant Colonel George Armstrong Custer led an expedition that confirmed the presence of gold on Sioux land. As settlers rushed for the gold, President Grant secretly ordered the military to stand down from its role as the Sioux Reservation's protector.

A majority of the Supreme Court ruled in favor of the Sioux. Central to the decision was President Grant's duplicity, which a lower court summed up as follows: "A more ripe and rank case of dishonorable dealings will never, in all probability, be found in our history."

Justice Rehnquist's dissent offered a different historical perspective. He quoted the *Oxford History of the American People* for the proposition that Indians would "inflict cruelty without qualm" and would rob or kill anyone "if they thought they could get away with it." Considering the treachery on both sides, Justice Rehnquist believed that, instead of judging the situation by the light of "revisionist" history, that "both settlers and Indians [were] entitled to the benefit of the Biblical adjuration," quoted above.

*The members of the American rock band, The Byrds, early 1965
(unknown photographer, from KRLA Beat/Beat Publications, Inc.)*

THE OLD TESTAMENT: ECCLESIASTES

For everything there is a season, and a time for every
purpose under heaven.

In re Sawyer, 360 U.S. 622, 666 (1959) (Frankfurter, J., dissenting) (quoting Ecclesiastes 3:1, 7).

In 1952, Honolulu attorney Harriet Bouslog Sawyer represented members of the International Longshoremen's and Warehousemen's Union ("ILWU") who were charged with violating the Smith Act, which makes it a crime to advocate the violent overthrow of the government. At an ILWU meeting, while the case was pending, attorney Sawyer made a series of disparaging remarks about the trial that were overheard by a newspaper reporter. Among other things, the newspaper reporter heard Sawyer say "there's no such thing as a fair trial in a Smith Act case," and "[a]ll rules of evidence have to be scrapped or the government can't make a case." Based on the reporter's notes, the Hawaii Bar Association concluded that Sawyer's comments violated professional ethics, which require lawyers to maintain a "respectful attitude" toward the court.

The Bar Association disciplined Sawyer with a one-year suspension from the practice of law. The Supreme Court reversed the discipline. Writing for the majority, Justice Brennan pointed out the discipline's procedural flaws, including the uncertainty of whether Sawyer's remarks disparaged the Smith Act, as opposed to the judge. In that regard, Justice Brennan noted that lawyers remain "free to criticize the state of the law."

Justice Frankfurter's dissent rejected any suggestion a lawyer's disrespect might qualify as protected First Amendment speech. From Justice Frankfurter's perspective, the First Amendment was "no exception" to "the law of life enunciated by Ecclesiastes," quoted above. Indeed, according to Justice Frankfurter, that famous Bible passage included a specific lesson for attorneys who are professionally obligated to treat courts with respect: there is a "time to speak" and a "time to keep silence."

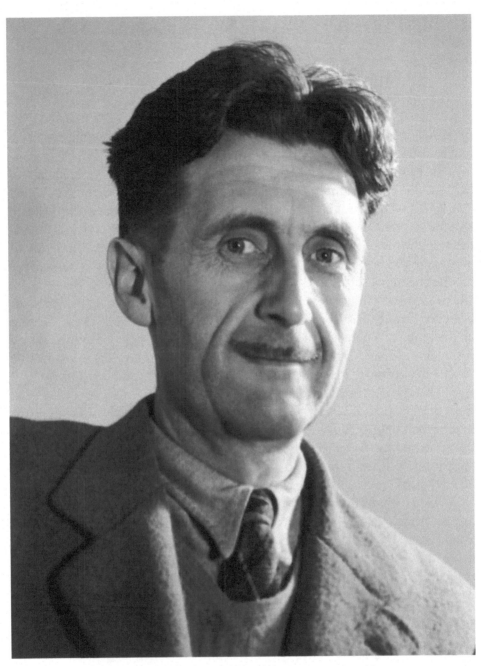

George Orwell, circa 1940 (unknown photographer)

GEORGE ORWELL

The black-mustachio'd face gazed down from every command-
ing corner. There was one on the house front immediately opposite. BIG BROTHER IS WATCHING YOU, the caption said....
In the far distance a helicopter skimmed down between the roofs,
hovered for an instant like a bluebottle, and darted away again
with a curving flight. It was the Police Patrol, snooping into
people's windows.

Florida v. Riley, 488 U.S. 445, 466 (1989) (Brennan, J., dissenting) (quoting
George Orwell, *Nineteen Eighty-Four* at page 4 (1949)).

If the police want to fly a helicopter over your house, and hover at 400
feet while engaging in surveillance of your property, must they first obtain a
warrant? That was the question in *Florida v. Riley*, which involved a mari-
juana growing operation in a greenhouse located behind a mobile home in
rural Pasco County Florida, north of Tampa.

A majority of the Supreme Court concluded no warrant was necessary
because the homeowner had no reasonable expectation of privacy from surveillance at that altitude. However, four Justices dissented, including Justice
Brennan, who likened the Florida Sheriff's helicopter surveillance to that of
the "Police Patrol" in George Orwell's classic novel.

Brutus and the Ghost of Caesar, 1802 (copperplate engraving by Edward Scriven from a painting by Richard Westfall, London)

WILLIAM SHAKESPEARE: JULIUS CAESAR

Come I to speak in Caesar's funeral.
He was my friend, faithful and just to me:
But Brutus says he was ambitious;
And Brutus is an honorable man.

Lakeside v. Oregon, 435 U.S. 333, 346 n.6 (1978) (Stevens, J., dissenting) (quoting William Shakespeare, *Julius Caesar*, Act III, Scene II).

In 1975, Ensio Ruben Lakeside was charged with escaping from Oregon's Multnomah County Correctional Institution. Lakeside decided not to testify in his own defense and, at the conclusion of the evidence, his lawyer objected to any Fifth Amendment jury instruction. The defense theory was that the prosecution failed to prove criminal intent, and Lakeside's attorney believed that a jury instruction on the right against self-incrimination would be "like waving a red flag in front of the jury." Nevertheless, over the defendant's objection, the trial judge instructed the jury not to draw any adverse inference from the defendant's failure to testify.

The jury convicted Lakeside, and the Supreme Court affirmed the conviction. Writing for the majority, Justice Stewart emphasized the trial judge's responsibility to conduct a fair trial without allowing defense counsel "the power to veto" jury instructions that were "wholly permissible."

Justice Stevens dissented. Identifying with the defendant's predicament, he argued that telling jurors to ignore a defendant's silence was "like telling them not to think of a white bear." For an illustration of how words can be used to suggest the opposite of their literal meaning, Justice Stevens quoted Marc Antony's funeral oration for Julius Caesar. Brutus, of course, had assassinated Caesar for being, among other things, overly "ambitious." In the funeral oration, Marc Antony sarcastically repeated the phrase "Brutus is an honorable man" in order to convey exactly the opposite message, which incited the crowd against Brutus.

William Shakespeare, English playwright and poet (Copper engraving by Martin Droeshout, Shakespeare - First Folio Faithfully Reproduced, Methuen, 1910)

WILLIAM SHAKESPEARE: HENRY 6TH

The first thing we do, let's kill all the lawyers.

Walters v. National Association of Radiation Survivors, 473 U.S. 305, 371 n.24 (1985) (Stevens, J., dissenting) (quoting William Shakespeare, *King Henry VI*, pt. II, Act IV, scene 2, line 72).

In 1862, due to the number of scoundrels practicing law at the time, Congress passed legislation limiting attorney fees in veteran pension benefit cases to $5. The law also imposed criminal penalties for any person who charged a veteran a fee in excess of that limitation. In 1864, Congress raised the cap to $10 and re-authorized the criminal penalties. Over the next 120 years, however, there was no change in the $10 cap or the criminal penalties, even though Congress developed an ever-more elaborate system for awarding veteran pension benefits. As a result, the law inhibited the ability to retain qualified legal counsel because of the difficulty of hiring a competent lawyer for such limited compensation.

In 1985, two veteran organizations asserted a constitutional challenge that reached the Supreme Court. Writing for the majority, Justice Rehnquist upheld the attorney fee limitations because the veteran pension benefit system was intended to be non-adversarial, so the addition of legal representation would only create more complexity and impose more costs, which ultimately would result in less money for veterans.

Justice Stevens dissented on the grounds the law interfered with a veteran's right to hire his own attorney at his own expense. According to Justice Stevens, the fee limitation could be upheld "[o]nly if it is assumed that the average lawyer is incompetent or unscrupulous," an assumption he notably rejected. For support, Justice Stevens quoted Shakespeare's famous line, which is "often misunderstood," since it was "spoken by a rebel, not a friend of liberty." As Justice Stevens explained, "Shakespeare insightfully realized that disposing of lawyers is a step in the direction of a totalitarian form of government."

Lear and Cordelia, illustrating Shakespeare's play King Lear, *circa 1849–54 (painting by Ford Madox Brown)*

WILLIAM SHAKESPEARE: KING LEAR

Why bastard, wherefore base?
When my dimensions are as well compact,
My mind as generous, and my shape as true,
As honest madam's issue?
Why brand they us with base?
With baseness? Bastardy? Base, base?

Levy v. Louisiana, 391 U.S. 68, 72 n.6 (1968) (Douglas, J.) (quoting William Shakespeare, *King Lear*, Act I, Scene 2).

Louise Levy was the mother of five illegitimate children who lived with her in Louisiana. Levy raised the children as a parent; she supported them by working as a domestic servant; and she paid for them to attend parochial school. But when Levy died, and the children sued Levy's doctor for wrongful death, the case was dismissed because the Louisiana wrongful death statute allowed such claims to be asserted only by legitimate children. The statutory distinction was based on "morals and general welfare," and its stated purpose was to discourage "bringing children into the world out of wedlock."

The Supreme Court reversed based on the Fourteenth Amendment's Equal Protection Clause. Writing for the majority, Justice Douglas explained that while a State may exercise its broad authority to make classifications, the distinctions may not be irrational or constitute "invidious discrimination" against a particular class. But in Levy's case, legitimacy of birth had "no relation" to the wrong allegedly inflicted on the mother, and the children took "no action" that was possibly relevant to the mother's injury.

To illustrate his point further, Justice Douglas offered the quote above from Shakespeare's King Lear, which questions the stigma attached to a bastard, even though his mind was as "generous" and his shape was as "true" as an "honest madam's issue."

*'Measure for Measure', Act II, Scene I, the Examination of Froth and Clown
by Escalus and Justice (from the Boydell series), [no date] (painting by
Robert Smirke)*

WILLIAM SHAKESPEARE: MEASURE FOR MEASURE

His acts did not o'ertake his bad intent;
And must be buried but as an intent
That perish'd by the way: thoughts are no subjects,
Intents but merely thoughts.

United States v. Apfelbaum, 445 U.S. 115, 132 (1980) (Rehnquist, J.) (quoting William Shakespeare, *Measure for Measure*, Act V, Scene 1; Glanville Williams, *Criminal Law*, The General Part 1 (2nd ed. 1961)).

Stanley Apfelbaum was subpoenaed to appear before a Grand Jury to testify about a robbery, but he refused based on his Fifth Amendment privilege against self-incrimination. In response, the government immunized Apfelbaum, which removed the grounds for Apfelbaum to invoke the Fifth Amendment. Nevertheless, if an immunized witness testifies and lies under oath, he may still be prosecuted for perjury, which is what happened to Apfelbaum. Apfelbaum appealed his perjury conviction on the grounds that the scope of his immunity should have applied to any subsequent prosecution, including perjury.

The Supreme Court disagreed because, at the time of the immunity, Apfelbaum had not yet perjured himself. Instead, at that time, Apfelbaum had, at most, thought about committing perjury, but "mere thoughts" are not criminal. Simply put, a crime is not committed unless thoughts are combined with action, as Justice Rehnquist illustrated with the above Shakespearean quote.

Shylock After the Trial, depicting Act II, Scene VII of Shakespeare's play
The Merchant of Venice, *pre-1873 (painting by Sir John Gilbert)*

WILLIAM SHAKESPEARE:
THE MERCHANT OF VENICE

> Yes, truly, for look you, the sins of the father are to be
> laid upon the children.

Tison v. Arizona, 481 U.S. 137, 184 n.20 (1987) (Brennan, J., dissenting) (quoting William Shakespeare, *The Merchant of Venice*, Act III, scene 5, line 1).

In 1978, Gary Tison escaped from an Arizona State Prison with the help of his three sons, Donald, Ricky, and Raymond. As the sons drove their fugitive father through the desert toward Flagstaff, a tire blew out, so they decided to flag down a passing motorist and steal a car. Raymond stood in front of the Tisons' car while the others hid. Eventually, a Mazda pulled over, which was occupied by John and Donnelda Lyons, their two-year-old son, and their fifteen-year-old niece. The Lyons family was forced into the backseat of the Tisons' car and taken to a more remote location, away from the highway. When John Lyons began to beg for his life, Gary Tison told his three sons to walk back to the Mazda to get some water. As they did, they heard their father shoot and kill the Lyons family. Eventually the police caught Ricky and Raymond Tison, who were tried and convicted and sentenced to death. Donald Tison and his father Gary were never prosecuted because they died trying to escape from the police manhunt.

The issue for the Supreme Court was whether the death penalty was constitutionally permissible even though Ricky and Raymond did not specifically intend to kill the Lyons family, and they did not inflict the fatal gunshot wounds. A majority of the Court concluded the death penalty was constitutional if the defendants were recklessly indifferent to human life and were major participants in the crime, which was supported by the record.

Justice Brennan dissented. He emphasized the murders were committed, not by the sons, but by the father, who was now dead. Justice Brennan's dissent criticized the "urge" to employ the death penalty against accomplices "when the killings stir public passion and the actual murderer is beyond human grasp." Quoting Shakespeare's Merchant of Venice, Justice Brennan wondered whether the "urge" was also "deeply rooted in our consciousness" that sons "must sometimes be punished for the sins of the father."

Ira Aldridge as Othello, circa 1830 (painting by Henry Perronet Briggs)

WILLIAM SHAKESPEARE: OTHELLO

Who steals my purse steals trash;
'Tis something, nothing;
'Twas mine, 'tis his, and has been slave to thousands;

But he that filches from me my good name
Robs me of that which not enriches him,
And makes me poor indeed.

Milkovich v. Lorain Journal Co., 497 U.S. 1, 12 (1990) (Rehnquist, C.J.)
(quoting William Shakespeare, *Othello*, Act III, scene 3).

In libel law, when a newspaper publishes an article accusing someone
of perjury, does it matter whether the article may be characterized as mere
"opinion"? No, explained Chief Justice Rehnquist, writing for the majority
in *Milkovich*.

The underlying controversy began at a Maple Heights High School
wrestling meet, in Cleveland, on February 8, 1974, when unruly fans
attacked and injured members of a rival team. The Ohio High School
Athletic Association disciplined the Maple Heights team and its coach,
Michael Milkovich, but a state court overturned the discipline. The next
day, the local newspaper published an article accusing Milkovich of lying
during the state court proceedings. According to the article, Milkovich
falsely testified he was "powerless to control the crowd" when, according to
the article, Milkovich was actually ranting and raving and egging on the
crowd. When Milkovich sued the paper for defamation, his case was dismissed on summary judgment on the grounds that the article was constitutionally protected "opinion."

The Supreme Court disagreed. After surveying the previously established categories of First Amendment protection, the Court declined to
create a new category for matters of "opinion." While recognizing the First
Amendment's "vital guarantee of free and uninhibited discussion of public
issues," Chief Justice Rehnquist explained there was "another side to the
equation"—that society has a strong interest in "redressing attacks upon
reputation." To illustrate the value of one's reputation, the Chief Justice
offered Iago's observations to Othello, quoted above.

Romeo and Juliet, between 1869 and 1870 (painting by Ford Madox Brown, Samuel and Mary R. Bancroft Memorial, 1935)

WILLIAM SHAKESPEARE:
ROMEO AND JULIET

What's in a name?

Dames & Moore v. Regan, 453 U.S. 654, 675, n.7 (1981) (Rehnquist, J.) (quoting William Shakespeare, *Romeo and Juliet*, Act II, scene 2, line 43).

When the government names a statute, it's natural to question the motive.

Sometimes the name has political overtones, as in the USA PATRIOT Act, which stands for "the Uniting and Strengthening America by Providing Appropriate Tools Required to Intercept and Obstruct Terrorism Act of 2001," Pub. L. 107-56, October 26, 2001. Other times, the statutory name is more of a marketing device, such as the BABIES Act, which is a less-than-perfect abbreviation for "the Bathrooms Accessible in Every Situation Act," Pub. L. 114-235, October 7, 2016.

The motive behind a statutory name was questioned in *Dames and Moore*, in which the Supreme Court upheld the government's power to transfer frozen assets to Iran, as part of a settlement of the 1979 Iranian hostage crisis. In that case, the Court upheld the government's authority based primarily on the sweeping language in the International Emergency Economic Powers Act, Pub. L. 95-223, December 28, 1977.

The government, however, also relied on an unnamed 100-year-old statute "concerning the Rights of American Citizens in foreign States." In an effort to refresh that old statute, the government's lawyers referred to it as "The Hostage Act." But that moniker was not well-received by Judge Mikva of the U.S. Court of Appeals for the District of Columbia Circuit. According to Judge Mikva, the government was only using that name as "a sobriquet newly coined for the purposes of the Iranian crisis."

Thankfully, when the case reached the Supreme Court, the name-calling ended. Writing for the majority, Justice Rehnquist acknowledged Judge Mikva's criticism while insisting the Justices focused their attention on the statutory wording, "not any shorthand description of it." In further pushback against the government's name game, Justice Rehnquist relied on the famous line from Shakespeare's tale of star-crossed lovers, quoted above.

Alfred Tennyson, English poet, 19th century (portrait by P. Krämer)

ALFRED TENNYSON

Theirs not to reason why,
theirs but to do and die.

Great-West Life & Annuity Ins. Co. v. Knudson, 534 U.S. 204, 223 (2002) (Stevens, J., dissenting) (quoting Alfred Tennyson, "The Charge of the Light Brigade").

The Supreme Court Justices often disagree about the extent to which Congressional intent should be taken into account when interpreting federal statutes. In *Great-West*, the Court struggled with a statute that, inexplicably, provided only limited relief to victims of pension fraud.

Writing for the majority, Justice Scalia argued it was improper to speculate about whether the legislative omission was deliberate.

In dissent, Justice Stevens insisted that, when faced with such an unreasonable situation, it was prudent for the Court to "pause and ask why," in contrast to the blind loyalty of the Crimean War soldiers Tennyson described in his famous poem.

Thoreau's Cove, Concord, Mass., circa 1908 (unknown photographer, Detroit Publishing Co.)

HENRY DAVID THOREAU

I have met with but one or two persons in the course of my life
who understood the art of Walking....

Papachristou v. City of Jacksonville, 405 U.S. 156, 165 n.7 (1972)
(Douglas, J.) (quoting Henry David Thoreau, *Excursions* 251–52 (1893)).

In Jacksonville, Florida, it was a crime to be a "rogue[] and vaga-
bond," or a "common night walker[]," or a "habitual loafer[]," who was
"wandering or strolling around from place to place without any lawful purpose." It was a typical example of a so-called vagrancy law, which was
common throughout the United States, with historical roots dating back to
the 16th Century Elizabethan poor laws.

In *Papachristou*, the Supreme Court declared Jacksonville's ordinance
"void for vagueness" because it failed to provide clear notice of the conduct
that was prohibited. Writing for the majority, Justice Douglas criticized the
loose statutory text, which allowed for too much prosecutorial discretion.
Or, as Justice Douglas more colorfully expressed it, upholding such a law
would mean the poor and the unpopular would be permitted to stand on the
public sidewalk "only at the whim of [a] police officer."

In the course of analyzing the statutory text, Justice Douglas took a
small detour to express his particular displeasure with the law's disparage-
ment of "walkers" and "wanderers." He pointed out that walking and
wandering were classic American traits, which had been extolled in poetry,
such as Walt Whitman's "Song of the Open Road," and Vachel Lindsay's "I
Want to Go Wandering." Continuing his literary frolic, Justice Douglas
offered the passage, quoted above, from Henry David Thoreau, who
glorified "the art of walking" as a "sort of crusade."

Mark Twain (Samuel Langhorne Clemens), circa 1907
(© A.F. Bradley, published in the "Famous People" chapter of the
ebook Great Photographs *from the Library of Congress, 2013)*

MARK TWAIN

The more you explain it, the more I don't understand it.

Securities and Exchange Commission v. Chenery Corp., 332 U.S. 194, 214 (1947) (Jackson, J., dissenting) (quoting Mark Twain, the pen name of Samuel Langhorne Clemens).

In *Chenery*, the Securities and Exchange Commission ("SEC") ordered sixteen corporate officers and directors to return various shares of preferred stock they had purchased on the open market. When the case reached the Supreme Court, a majority of Justices ruled in favor of the officers and directors and remanded the case to the SEC for further consideration. On remand, the SEC "recast its rationale," but "reached the same result." The officers and directors again took their case to the Supreme Court, but this time a majority of the Justices ruled in favor of the SEC. To explain the flip-flop, the Supreme Court asserted it was not allowed to affirm agency action that may be right for the wrong reasons. Instead, the agency must articulate the proper rationale. That explanation, however, failed to satisfy Justice Jackson, who chided the result with Mark Twain's adage.

Tom Sawyer, U.S. commemorative 8-cent stamp of 1972
(designed by Bradbury Thompson)

MARK TWAIN

It is by the goodness of God that in our country
we have those three unspeakably precious things:
freedom of speech, freedom of conscience,
and the prudence never to practice either of them.

Scales v. United States, 367 U.S. 203, 262–63 (1961) (Douglas, J., dissenting) (quoting Mark Twain, *Following the Equator* (1903), Vol. I, p. 198).

In 1955, Junius Irving Scales was convicted of violating the "membership clause" of the Smith Act, which made it a crime, punishable by up to twenty years in prison, to affiliate with a group while knowing that its purpose was to teach, advocate or encourage the government's violent overthrow.

Scales was the Chairman of the North and South Carolina Districts of the Communist Party; he recruited new members; and he promoted the Communist education of young Party members at secret schools, including one where he was the Director. He also distributed literature that Communism's goals could only be achieved by a working-class violent revolution.

In a 5-4 decision, the Supreme Court upheld Scales's conviction. The Court concluded the Smith Act's "membership clause" was Constitutional as long as the prosecution was limited to defendants who were "active" members with "specific intent" to further the organization's prohibited purposes.

Justice Douglas dissented. From his perspective, in the absence of any unlawful overt act, the majority was condoning "guilt by association." In light of the potential chilling effect on First Amendment rights, Justice Douglas quipped that the majority's decision "make[s] serious Mark Twain's lighthearted comment," quoted above.

Aeneas' Ship Landing on an Island, 1483 (illustration pictured in the French edition of Virgil's Aeneid, *published in Lyon by Guillaume Le Roy)*

VIRGIL

Insula portum efficit objectu laterum,
quibus omnis ab alto frangitur,
inque sinus scindit sese unda reductos.

United States v. Rodgers, 150 U.S. 249, 286 n.1 (1893) (Field, J.) (quoting Virgil, *The Aeneid*, Book 1).

Does anyone miss the days when a Supreme Court Justice felt free to make a legal point by quoting Virgil's *Aeneid* in Latin?

It hasn't happened since 1893, when Justice Field relied on that classic to resolve an issue of criminal jurisdiction. The issue was whether a federal criminal statute applied to an assault aboard a steamer operating in the Great Lakes. Pursuant to the statute, jurisdiction depended in part on whether the Great Lakes qualified as the "high seas."

Writing for the majority, Justice Field concluded the answer was yes, based in part on the passage quoted above, which translates as follows:

There an island's deep bay forms a harbor with its sides.
Every wave from the high sea is broken here
and fans out to the curving coves.

(*The Aeneid*, translated by Shadi Bartsch, Random House 2021).

The passage comes from the epic poem's opening scene, when Aeneas and his crew escaped the Trojan War, sailed across the Mediterranean, and found safe harbor in Carthage. Justice Field relied on the passage to demonstrate, in essence, that if the Mediterranean qualified as the "high sea," then so did the Great Lakes.

But why would Justice Field go so far for such a small point?

The likely answer is that Justice Field was having a so-called "Rosebud" moment: he was reminiscing about his own childhood trip along a similar route as Aeneas. At the age of thirteen, Field joined members of his family on a mission to the Greek isles, and the Turkish coast, in the vicinity of the mythic city of Troy. As Justice Field's biographers pointed out, that childhood Mediterranean journey had a "deep and lasting impression" on the future Justice's "intellectual and moral character" (John Norton Pomeroy, *Some Account of the Work of Stephen J. Field as a Legislator, State Judge, and Judge of the Supreme Court of the United States*, The Lawbook Exchange, Ltd. 2003).

Kurt Vonnegut, [1965] (photograph by Bernard Gotfryd)

KURT VONNEGUT

The year was 2001, and "everybody was finally equal."

PGA Tour, Inc. v. Martin, 532 U.S. 661, 705 (2001) (Scalia, J., dissenting) (quoting Kurt Vonnegut's essay "Harrison Bergeron," in *Animal Farm and Related Readings* at page 129 (1997)).

Casey Martin was a professional golfer who suffered from a degenerative circulatory disorder that made it difficult for him to walk long distances. As a result of his disability, Martin requested permission to use a motorized cart during professional golf tournaments, even though the rules required all competitors to walk. The Professional Golf Association rejected the request, and Martin sued. The Supreme Court concluded that, as applied to Martin, the rule prohibiting the use of a golf cart in a professional tournament violated the Americans with Disabilities Act.

In a scathing dissent, Justice Scalia accused the majority of engaging in "Kafkaesque" judicial reasoning in which there was one set of rules for "able-bodied" athletes and another set of rules for "talented but disabled athletes." Justice Scalia's dissent concluded by borrowing the phrase, quoted above, from Kurt Vonnegut's satirical essay "Harrison Bergeron," which begins with the following paragraph:

> The year was 2081, and everybody was finally equal. They weren't only equal before God and the law. They were equal every which way. Nobody was smarter than anybody else. Nobody was better looking than anybody else. Nobody was stronger or quicker than anybody else. All this equality was due to the 211th, 212th, and 213th Amendments to the Constitution, and to the unceasing vigilance of agents of the United States Handicapper General.

GLOSSARY

Affirm. "In the practice of appellate courts, to *affirm* a judgment, decree, or order is to declare that it is valid and right and must stand as rendered below." *Black's Law Dictionary* 55 (5th ed. 1979) (emphasis in original).

Americans with Disabilities Act. The Americans with Disabilities Act of 1990, 104 Stat. 328, 42 U.S.C. § 12101 *et seq.*, prohibits certain employers from discriminating against individuals on the basis of their disabilities. *Sutton v. United Air Lines, Inc.*, 527 U.S. 471, 475 (1999) (O'Connor, J.).

Cease and desist order. "An order of an administrative agency or court prohibiting a person or business firm from continuing a particular course of conduct." *Black's Law Dictionary* 202 (5th ed. 1979).

Chief Justice ("C.J."). "The presiding, most senior, or principal judge of a court." *Black's Law Dictionary* 216 (5th ed. 1979).

Clean Water Act. Congress passed the Clean Water Act to establish an all-encompassing program of water pollution regulation. *City of Milwaukee v. Illinois and Michigan,* 451 U.S. 304, 318 (1981) (Rehnquist, J.).

Conscientious objector. "One who, by reason of religious training and belief, is conscientiously opposed to participation in war." *Black's Law Dictionary* 275 (5th ed. 1979).

Contempt. "A willful disregard or disobedience of a public authority." *Black's Law Dictionary* 288 (5th ed. 1979).

Dissent. "The term is most commonly used to denote the explicit disagreement of one or more judges of a court with the decision passed by the majority upon a case before them. In such event, the non-concurring judge is reported as 'dissenting.'" *Black's Law Dictionary* 424 (5th ed. 1979).

Due Process Clause. "Two such clauses are found in the U.S. Constitution, one in the 5th Amendment pertaining to the federal government, the other in the 14th Amendment which protects persons from state actions. There are two aspects: procedural, in which a person is guaranteed fair procedures, and substantive which protects a person's property from unfair governmental interference or taking." *Black's Law Dictionary* 449 (5th ed. 1979).

En banc. "Refers to a session where the entire membership of the court will participate in the decision rather than the regular quorum." *Black's Law Dictionary* 472–73 (5th ed. 1979).

Equal Protection Clause. "That provision in the 14th Amendment to U.S. Constitution which prohibits a State from denying to any person within its jurisdiction the equal protection of the laws." *Black's Law Dictionary* 481 (5th ed. 1979).

Establishment Clause. "That provision of the First Amendment to U.S. Constitution which provides that 'Congress shall make no law respecting an establishment of religion, or prohibiting the free exercise thereof....'" *Black's Law Dictionary* 490 (5th ed. 1979).

Fifth Amendment. "Amendment to U.S. Constitution providing that no person shall be required to answer for a capital or otherwise infamous offense unless on indictment or presentment of a grand jury except in military cases; that no person will suffer double jeopardy; that no person will be compelled to be a witness against himself; that no person shall be deprived of life, liberty or property without due process of law and that property will not be taken for public use without just compensation." *Black's Law Dictionary* 565 (5th ed. 1979).

First Amendment. "Amendment to U.S. Constitution guaranteeing basic freedoms of speech, religion, press, and assembly and the right to petition the government for redress of grievances." *Black's Law Dictionary* 571 (5th ed. 1979).

Freedom of speech. "Right guaranteed by First Amendment of U.S. Constitution." *Black's Law Dictionary* 598 (5th ed. 1979).

Gideon v. Wainwright. "Landmark Supreme Court decision which held that provision guaranteeing a criminal defendant the assistance of counsel under the Sixth Amendment, U.S. Constitution, is binding on the states in state proceedings through the due process provision of the Fourteenth Amendment." *Black's Law Dictionary* 619 (5th ed. 1979).

Indictment. "An accusation in writing found and presented by a grand jury, legally convoked and sworn, to the court in which it is impaneled, charging that a person therein named has done some act, or been guilty of some omission, which by law is a public offense, punishable on indictment." *Black's Law Dictionary* 695 (5th ed. 1979).

Judgment lien. "A lien binding on the real estate of a judgment debtor, in favor of the holder of the judgment, and giving the latter a right to levy on the land for the satisfaction of his judgment to the exclusion of other adverse interests subsequent to the judgment." *Black's Law Dictionary* 758 (5th ed. 1979).

Majority opinion. "The opinion of an appellate court in which the majority of its members join." *Black's Law Dictionary* 860 (5th ed. 1979).

Mandatory minimum. In the 1970s and 1980s, as part of a national effort to enact tougher sentences, legislatures passed mandatory minimum sentencing laws, which had the effect of imposing mandatory limits on a sentencing judge's discretion. *United States v. O'Brien*, 560 U.S. 218, 235–36 (2010) (Stevens, J., concurring).

Nuisance. "Nuisance is that activity which arises from unreasonable, unwarranted or unlawful use by a person of his own property, working obstruction or injury to right of another, or to the public, and producing such material annoyance, inconvenience and discomfort that law will presume resulting damage." *Black's Law Dictionary* 961 (5th ed. 1979).

Obscene. "Objectionable or offensive to accepted standards of decency." *Black's Law Dictionary* 971 (5th ed. 1979).

Per curiam. Latin for "By the Court. A phrase used to distinguish an opinion of the whole court from an opinion written by any one judge." *Black's Law Dictionary* 1023 (5th ed. 1979).

Plurality. "An opinion of an appellate court in which more justices join than in any concurring opinion (though not a majority of the court) is a plurality opinion as distinguished from a majority opinion in which a larger number of the justices on the panel join than not." *Black's Law Dictionary* 1039 (5th ed. 1979).

Remand. "The sending by the appellate court of the cause back to the same court out of which it came, for the purpose of having some further action taken on it there." *Black's Law Dictionary* 1162 (5th ed. 1979).

Search warrant. "An order in writing, issued by a justice or other magistrate, in the name of the state, directed to a sheriff, constable, or other officer, authorizing him to search for and seize any property that constitutes evidence of the commission of a crime, contraband, the fruits of crime, or things otherwise criminally possessed; or, property designed or intended for use or which is or has been used as the means of committing a crime. A warrant may be issued upon an affidavit or sworn oral testimony." *Black's Law Dictionary* 1211 (5th ed. 1979).

Separation of powers. "The governments of states and the United States are divided into three departments or branches: the legislative, which is empowered to make laws, the executive which is required to carry out the laws, and the judicial which is charged with interpreting the laws and adjudicating disputes under the laws. One branch is not permitted to encroach on the domain of another." *Black's Law Dictionary* 1225 (5th ed. 1979).

Smith Act. "Federal law which punishes, among other activities, the advocacy of the overthrow of the government by force or violence." *Black's Law Dictionary* 1246 (5th ed. 1979).

Standing to sue doctrine. "'Standing to sue' means that party has sufficient stake in an otherwise justiciable controversy to obtain judicial resolution of that controversy." *Black's Law Dictionary* 1260 (5th ed. 1979).

Stare decisis. Latin for "to abide by, or adhere to, decided cases." *Black's Law Dictionary* 1261 (5th ed. 1979).

Tax lien. "A statutory lien, existing in favor of the state or municipality, upon the lands of a person charged with taxes, finding the same either for the taxes assessed upon the specific track or land or (in some jurisdictions) for all the taxes due from the individual, and which may be foreclosed for non-payment, by judgment of a court or sale of the land." *Black's Law Dictionary* 1308 (5th ed. 1979).

Three Strikes laws. Starting in the 1990s, "three strikes laws effected a sea change in criminal sentencing throughout the Nation. These laws responded to widespread public concerns about crime by targeting the class of offenders who pose the greatest threat to public safety: career criminals." *Ewing v. California*, 538 U.S. 11, 24 (2003) (O'Connor, J.) (footnote omitted).

Uniform Code of Military Justice. "The body of law which governs military persons in their conduct as military personnel." *Black's Law Dictionary* 1373 (5th ed. 1979).

Vacate. "To annul; to set aside; to cancel or rescind. To render an act void; as, to vacate an entry of record, or a judgment." *Black's Law Dictionary* 1388 (5th ed. 1979).

The Voting Rights Act. "Federal Act (1965) which suspended all literacy and character tests for voting rights in all States and counties where less than half the adult population were registered, and which provided for federal regulation of voters where the Attorney General considered it necessary to enforce rights under the 15th Amendment." *Black's Law Dictionary* 1414 (5th ed. 1979).

Writ of certiorari. "An order by the appellate court which is used when the court has discretion on whether or not to hear an appeal. If the writ is denied, the court refuses to hear an appeal and, in effect, the judgment below stands unchanged. If the writ is granted, then it has the effect of ordering the lower court to certify the record and send it up to the higher court which has used its discretion to hear the appeal." *Black's Law Dictionary* 1443 (5th ed. 1979).

CROSS-INDEX OF THE JUSTICES
AND THEIR QUOTES

Justice Samuel Alito

"Imagine all the people, living life in peace." *Pleasant Grove City v. Summum*, 555 U.S. 460, 475 n.2 (2009) (Alito, J.) (quoting John Lennon, "Imagine," on *Imagine* (Apple Records 1971)).

"In Flanders fields the poppies blow, between the crosses, row on row." *American Legion v. American Humanist Association*, 139 S. Ct. 2067, 2075–76 (2019) (Alito, J.) (quoting John McCrae's poem in *Flanders Fields and Other Poems* 3 (G.P. Putnam's Sons ed. 1919)).

Justice Hugo Black

"He who rises against Germany is a traitor to his country...." *Jay v. Boyd*, 351 U.S. 345, 369 n. 12 (1956) (Black, J., dissenting) (quoting Adolph Hitler's July 13, 1934 Reichstag speech, as quoted in 1 *Hitler's Speeches* (Baynes ed. 1942) 321–24)).

Justice Harry Blackmun

"Tinker to Evers to Chance." *Flood v. Kuhn*, 407 U.S. 258, 264 n.5 (1972) (Blackmun, J.) (quoting Franklin Pierce Adams, "Baseball's Sad Lexicon").

"No man is an island." *Sierra Club v. Morton*, 405 U.S. 727, 760, n.2 (1972) (Blackmun, J., dissenting) (quoting John Donne, *Devotions* XVII).

Justice William Brennan

"The man who enjoys his coffee while reading that justice has been done would spit it out at the least detail." *Glass v. Louisiana*, 471 U.S. 1080, 1087 n.12 (1985) (Brennan, J., dissenting) (quoting Albert Camus, "Reflections on the Guillotine," *Resistance, Rebellion, and Death* 187 (1961)).

"[Hercules] now set out to perform his fifth Labour, and this time his task was to cleanse the stables of Augeas in a single day." *Sakraida v. Ag Pro, Inc.*, 425 U.S. 273, 275 n.1 (1976) (Brennan, J.) (quoting C. Witt, *Classic Mythology* 119–20 (1883)).

"BIG BROTHER IS WATCHING YOU." *Florida v. Riley*, 488 U.S. 445, 466 (1989) (Brennan, J., dissenting) (quoting George Orwell, *Nineteen Eighty-Four* at p. 4 (1949)).

"… the sins of the father are to be laid upon the children." *Tison v. Arizona*, 481 U.S. 137, 184 n.20 (1987) (Brennan, J., dissenting) (quoting William Shakespeare, *The Merchant of Venice*, Act III, scene 5, line 1).

Justice Stephen Breyer

"Before I built a wall I'd ask to know what I was walling in or walling out." *Plaut v. Spendthrift Farm, Inc.*, 514 U.S. 211, 245 (1995) (Breyer, J., concurring) (quoting Robert Frost, "Mending Wall," *The New Oxford Book of American Verse* 395–96 (R. Ellmann ed. 1976)).

Justice William Douglas

"I will not sign." *Gibson v. Florida Legislative Investigation Committee*, 372 U.S. 539, 574–75 (1963) (Douglas, J., concurring) (quoting Robert Bolt, *A Man for All Seasons* (1960), pp. 132–33).

"The law, in its majestic equality, forbids the rich as well as the poor, to sleep under bridges, to beg in the streets, and to steal bread." *Reck v. Pate*, 367 U.S. 433, 446 n.5 (1961) (Douglas, J., concurring) (quoting Anatole France, as quoted in Cournos, *A Modern Plutarch* (1928), p. 27).

"I have met with but one or two persons in the course of my life who understood the art of Walking…." *Papachristou v. City of Jacksonville*, 405 U.S. 156, 165 n.7 (1972) (Douglas, J.) (quoting Henry David Thoreau, *Excursions* 251–52 (1893)).

"It is by the goodness of God that in our country we have those three unspeakably precious things: freedom of speech, freedom of conscience, and the prudence never to practice either of them." *Scales v. United States*, 367 U.S. 203, 262–63 (1961) (Douglas, J., dissenting) (quoting Mark Twain, *Following the Equator* (1903), Vol. I, p. 198).

"Now as he journeyed he approached Damascus, and suddenly a light from heaven flashed about him." *Ehlert v. United States*, 402 U.S. 99, 108 & n.2 (1971) (Douglas, J., dissenting) (quoting the New Testament, 9 Acts 3–6 (rev. Standard ed. 1952)).

"Why bastard, wherefore base?" *Levy v. Louisiana*, 391 U.S. 68, 72 n.6 (1968) (Douglas, J.) (quoting William Shakespeare, *King Lear*, Act I, Scene 2).

Justice Stephen Field

"Insula portum efficit objectu laterum, quibus omnis ab alto frangitur, inque sinus scindit sese unda reductos." *United States v. Rodgers*, 150 U.S. 249, 286 n.1 (1893) (Field, J.) (quoting Virgil, *The Aeneid*, Book 1).

Justice Felix Frankfurter

"For everything there is a season, and a time for every purpose under heaven." *In re Sawyer*, 360 U.S. 622, 666 (1959) (Frankfurter, J., dissenting) (quoting Ecclesiastes 3:1, 7).

Justice Ruth Bader Ginsburg

"I will not carry a gun." *Muscarello v. United States*, 524 U.S. 125, 144 n.6 (1998) (Ginsburg, J., dissenting) (quoting Alan Alda playing the role of Hawkeye Pierce in the television series "M*A*S*H").

"Herald, read the accusation!" *Nelson v. Adams USA, Inc.*, 529 U.S. 460, 468 n.2 (2000) (Ginsburg, J.) (quoting Lewis Carroll, *Alice in Wonderland and Through the Looking Glass* 108 (Messner 1982)).

Justice Robert Jackson

"The more you explain it, the more I don't understand it." *Securities and Exchange Commission v. Chenery Corp.*, 332 U.S. 194, 214 (1947) (Jackson, J., dissenting) (quoting Mark Twain).

Justice Elena Kagan

"[I]n this world, with great power there must also come—great responsibility." *Kimble v. Marvel Entertainment, LLC*, 576 U.S. 446, 465 (2015) (Kagan, J.) (quoting Stan Lee & Steve Ditko, Amazing Fantasy No. 15: "Spider-Man," p. 13 (1962)).

Justice Anthony Kennedy

"… we pray to Buddha and all other Gods." *Town of Greece v. Galloway*, 572 U.S. 565, 579 (2014) (Kennedy, J.) (quoting the Dalai Lama's March 6,

2014 opening prayer to the U.S. Congress, as reported in 160 Cong. Rec. S1329).

Justice Thurgood Marshall

"... [P]eople understand one another with difficulty unless talking face to face." *Kleindienst v Mandel*, 408 U.S. 53, 776 n.2 (1972) (Marshall, J., dissenting) (quoting Albert Einstein, as quoted in Developments in the Law—The National Security Interest and Civil Liberties, 85 Harv. L. Rev. 1130, 1154 (1972)).

"Whether Leviathan can long endure so wide a chase...." *Japan Whaling Association v. American Cetacean Society*, 478 U.S. 221, 249–50 (1986) (Marshall, J., dissenting) (quoting Herman Melville, *Moby Dick* 436 (Signet ed. 1961)).

Chief Justice William Rehnquist

"There are three kinds of lies: lies, damned lies, and statistics." *Procter & Gamble Mfg. Co. v. Fisher*, 449 U.S. 1115, 1118 (1981) (Rehnquist, J., dissenting) (quoting nineteenth century British Prime Minister Benjamin Disraeli).

"And fired the shot heard 'round the world." *Texas v. Johnson*, 491 U.S. 397, 422 (1989) (Rehnquist, C.J, dissenting) (quoting Ralph Waldo Emerson's "Concord Hymn").

"Judge not, that ye be not judged." *United States v. Sioux Nation of Indians*, 448 U.S. 371, 437 (1980) (Rehnquist, J., dissenting) (quoting Matthew 7:1–3) (King James version).

"What's in a name?" *Dames & Moore v. Regan*, 453 U.S. 654, 675, n.7 (1981) (Rehnquist, J.) (quoting William Shakespeare, *Romeo and Juliet*, Act II, scene 2, line 43).

"... he that filches from me my good name robs me of that which not enriches him, and makes me poor indeed." *Milkovich v. Lorain Journal Co.*, 497 U.S. 1, 12 (1990) (Rehnquist, C.J.) (quoting William Shakespeare, *Othello*, Act III, scene 3).

"His acts did not o'ertake his bad intent." *United States v. Apfelbaum*, 445 U.S. 115, 132 (1980) (Rehnquist, J.) (quoting William Shakespeare, *Measure for Measure*, Act V, Scene 1; Glanville Williams, *Criminal Law*, The General Part 1 (2nd ed. 1961)).

"Judge not, that ye be not judged." *United States v. Sioux Nation of Indians*, 448 U.S. 371, 437 (1980) (Rehnquist, J., dissenting) (quoting Matthew 7:1–3, King James version).

Chief Justice John Roberts

"When you got nothing, you got nothing to lose." *Sprint Communications, Co., L.P. v. APCC Services, Inc.*, 554 U.S. 269, 301 (2008) (Roberts, C.J., dissenting) (quoting Bob Dylan, "Like a Rolling Stone," on *Highway 61 Revisited* (Columbia Records 1965)).

"Plenty of nothing." *Bank Markazi v. Peterson*, 136 S. Ct. 1310, 1335 (2016) (Roberts, C.J., dissenting) (quoting Ira Gershwin & DuBose Heyward, *Porgy and Bess*: Libretto 28 (1958)).

Justice Antonin Scalia

"I was misinformed." *Rapanos v. United States*, 547 U.S. 715, 727 n.2 (2006) (Scalia, J.) (quoting *Save Our Sonoran, Inc. v. Flowers*, 408 F.3d 1113, 1117 (9th Cir. 2005) (quoting the movie *Casablanca*, Warner Bros. 1942)).

"Even so did we seize the fiery-pointed brand and whirled it round in his eye, and the blood flowed about the heated bar." *Brown v. Entertainment Merchants Association*, 564 U.S. 786, 796 (2011) (Scalia, J.) (quoting *The Odyssey of Homer*, Book IX, p. 125 (S. Butcher & A. Lang transls. 1909)).

"The year was 2001, and 'everybody was finally equal.'" *PGA Tour, Inc. v. Martin*, 532 U.S. 661, 705 (2001) (Scalia, J., dissenting) (quoting Kurt Vonnegut's essay "Harrison Bergeron," in *Animal Farm and Related Readings* at page 129 (1997)).

Justice David Souter

"My object of living is 'to unite [m]y avocation and my vocation.'" *Garcetti v. Ceballos*, 547 U.S. 410, 432 at n.3 (2006) (Souter, J., dissenting) (quoting Robert Frost, Two Tramps in Mud Time, *Collected Poems, Prose & Plays* 251, 252 (R. Poirier & M. Richardson eds. 1995)).

Justice John Paul Stevens

"The dog that did not bark." *Chisom v. Roemer*, 501 U.S. 380, 396 n.23 (1991) (Stevens, J.) (citing Arthur Conan Doyle, Silver Blaze, in *The Complete Sherlock Holmes* 335 (1927)).

"In this world nothing can be said to be certain, except death and taxes." *U.S. v. Estate of Romani*, 523 U.S. 517, 520 n.2 (1988) (Stevens, J.) (quoting Benjamin Franklin's November 13, 1789 letter to Jean Baptiste LeRoy, as published in 10 *The Writings of Benjamin Franklin* 69 (A. Smyth ed. 1907)).

"Frankly, my dear, I don't give a damn." *Bethel School District Number 403 v. Fraser*, 478 U.S. 675, 691 (1986) (Stevens, J., dissenting) (quoting Clark Gable, as Rhett Butler, in the 1939 film *Gone with the Wind*).

"The first thing we do, let's kill all the lawyers." *Walters v. National Association of Radiation Survivors*, 473 U.S. 305, 371 n.24 (1985) (Stevens, J., dissenting) (quoting William Shakespeare, *King Henry VI*, pt. II, Act IV, scene 2, line 72).

"And Brutus is an honorable man." *Lakeside v. Oregon*, 435 U.S. 333, 346 n.6 (1978) (Stevens, J., dissenting) (quoting William Shakespeare, *Julius Caesar*, Act III, Scene II).

"Theirs not to reason why, theirs but to do and die." *Great-West Life & Annuity Ins. Co. v. Knudson*, 534 U.S. 204, 223 (2002) (Stevens, J., dissenting) (quoting Alfred Tennyson, "the Charge of the Light Brigade").

Justice Potter Stewart

"We accuse you also of the commission of crimes and infractions we don't even know about yet." *Parker v. Levy*, 417 U.S. 733, 788 n.41 (1974) (Stewart, J., dissenting) (quoting Joseph Heller, *Catch-22*, p. 395 (Dell ed. 1970)).

"… the rights of man come not from the generosity of the state but from the hand of God." *Engel v. Vitale*, 370 U.S. 421, 448 n.3 (1962) (Stewart, J., dissenting) (quoting John F. Kennedy's Inaugural Address, Jan. 20, 1961).

Justice Clarence Thomas

"In the long run we are all dead." *Tahoe-Sierra Preservation Council, Inc. v. Tahoe Regional Planning Agency*, 535 U.S. 302, 356 (2002) (Thomas, J., dissenting) (quoting John Maynard Keynes, *Monetary Reform* 88 (1924)).

Chief Justice Earl Warren

"Hell is paved with good intentions." *Burgett v. Texas*, 389 U.S. 109, 117 n.2 (1967) (Warren, C.J., concurring) (quoting James Boswell, *The Life of Samuel Johnson* 257 (Great Books ed. 1952)).

"An open foe may prove a curse, but a pretended friend is worse." *Spano v. People of the State of New York*, 360 U.S. 315, 323 (1959) (Warren, C.J.) (quoting John Gay).

TOPICAL INDEX

126

TABLE OF CASES